The Foreign Relations of India

Comparative Foreign Relations Series

Edited by
David O. Wilkinson
University of California, Los Angeles

Lawrence Scheinman
Cornell University

Comparative Foreign Relations: Framework and Methods
David O. Wilkinson, University of California, Los Angeles

The Foreign Relations of the United States, Second Edition
Michael H. Armacost, U.S. Department of State
Michael M. Stoddard, Pomona College

The Foreign Relations of China, Second Edition
Robert C. North, Stanford University

The Foreign Policy of the USSR: Domestic Factors
Morton Schwartz, University of California, Riverside

The Foreign Relations of India
Sudershan Chawla, California State University, Long Beach

Of Related Interest:

Latin America: Catholicism and Class Conflict
Lawrence Littwin, California State University, Northridge

American Foreign Policy in a Polycentric World, Second Edition
Douglas Mendel, University of Wisconsin, Milwaukee

Whose Country America? An Introductory Reader on American Politics   Philip C. Beardsley, Syracuse University

Realpolitik: Theory and Practice
Ira S. Cohen, California State University, Long Beach

Dickenson Publishing Company, Inc.
Encino, California & Belmont, California

The Foreign Relations of India

Sudershan Chawla
California State University,
Long Beach

Copyright © December 1976 by Dickenson Publishing Company, Inc. All rights reserved. No part of this book may be reproduced, stored in a retrieval system, or transcribed, in any form or by any means—electronic, mechanical, photocopying, recording, or otherwise—without the prior written permission of the publisher, 16250 Ventura Boulevard, Encino, California 91436.

ISBN-0-8221-0182-3
Library of Congress Catalog Card Number: 76-4356

Printed in the United States of America
Printing (last digit): 9 8 7 6 5 4 3 2 1

The author wishes to acknowledge use of material from the following sources:

From *India and World Politics* by Michael Brecher, © Oxford University Press, 1968. Reprinted by permission of the publisher.

From *India's Quest for Security: Defense Policies, 1947–1965* by Lorne J. Kavic. Copyright © 1967 by The Regents of the University of California, reprinted by permission of the University of California Press.

Cover by Preston J. Mitchell.

To Bhabiji and Pitaji

Contents

	Foreword	ix
	Preface	xi
1	Introduction	1
2	India's capability factor and foreign policy	12
3	Political beliefs, ideals, and historical traditions	47
4	Foreign policy formulation	57
5	India's political process: its influence on foreign policy	73
6	Some general characteristics of India's foreign policy	90
7	India and her neighbors	106
8	India and the "big three" powers	130
	Epilogue	150
	Appendix	154
	Index	161

Foreword

The COMPARATIVE FOREIGN RELATIONS SERIES is designed for foreign policy courses that employ a comparative approach, as well as for courses in comparative politics and international relations that survey the foreign relations of key states. Because the basic literature is lacking, few courses today are able to make a genuinely comparative examination of national actors in the international system, in the manner increasingly adopted for the study of domestic politics. This series has been prepared to fill the need for such a basic literature.

The series presents an analytical model and case materials for beginning a comparative study of foreign relations. As a method of studying foreign relations phenomena, comparison allows us to investigate the differences and similarities among states in relation to the international system, and thereby generate or test propositions about the external relations of states.

In order to compare cases, an analytical model or framework should be used—that is, the same set of subjects and questions should be used to arrange and present information about each case. The analytical model of the series is presented in the core volume, *Comparative Foreign Relations: Framework and Methods,* which outlines a framework for describing the international situation and foreign policy of a state, explaining its current policy, analyzing its current problems, and projecting its future problems and policy alternatives. The case materials are presented in the various country volumes, which, following the analytical model, describe and explain the foreign relations of specific important states since 1945 and sketch their main current and anticipated problems.

The books in the series make comparison possible by presenting material of the same nature about each case; however, the actual comparisons must be made by the reader. Some ways in which the series might be used to further the comparative study of foreign relations are presented in the preface to the core volume.

David O. Wilkinson
Lawrence Scheinman

Preface

The Foreign Relations of India attempts to acquaint the reader with the multiple dimensions of foreign policy and foreign policymaking. It is not a chronological diplomatic history of India, nor does it deal exclusively with India's foreign relations. Mainly, this book is a synthesis. While it is neither exhaustive nor all-encompassing, the analysis deals with the Indian government's foreign policymaking apparatus; the strategic, economic, and philosophical assumptions of the policymaking elites; and the major foreign policy goals of the Indian government since 1947.

As part of the COMPARATIVE FOREIGN RELATIONS SERIES, it follows the approach and organization suggested by the parent volume, *Comparative Foreign Relations: Framework and Methods*, by Professor David O. Wilkinson.

Much of the material covered in this volume was researched during a year (1971–72) spent in India. I received invaluable assistance from many sources while I was there. I owe special thanks to the Librarian at the Indian Council of World Affairs. I wish to thank Dr. Hari Vaishanav and Dr. J. P. Chawla, who arranged interviews for me which were most informative and helped in gaining an insight into India's foreign policy posture. I owe a great debt of gratitude to Vaid and Ram Batra of New Delhi who made available to me all the means necessary to carry out the research.

Without the constant encouragement and support of Professors Lawrence Scheinman and David Wilkinson, I would not have been able to complete the task. I am most grateful to them.

Sudershan Chawla

The Foreign Relations of India

1
Introduction

It is difficult to determine how much of the foreign policy of a state is the result of a design carved by the policymakers, and how much of it is the result of an attempt to adjust to circumstance. Factors like past experience, military and economic capability, and the current domestic and international situation no doubt all played their part in molding the final form of India's foreign policy. But a close examination reveals that certain influences, by no means all of them of India's own choosing, had a powerful impact on her policies. By the time India became independent in 1947, after a century and a half of foreign domination, the modern states of Europe had molded international politics into a legacy and an environment for both new and old states of the world. More than that, the tools of power and diplomacy that India could use to adjust her relations with other states were those which were bequeathed to her as a colony by her former masters. Thus, despite the indomitable will of India's first prime minister and foreign minister, Jawaharlal Nehru, the country's ability to maneuver on the international scene was severely circumscribed.

At the time of her independence, India's military and industrial capacity hardly permitted an active role in international politics. But policy making was primarily in the hands of one man, the late Prime Minister Nehru, who was determined to see that India make an impact on the world scene. The pattern of Indian foreign policy that surfaced in the first two and a half decades after independence reflects the actions and reactions of a strong-willed leadership working with a large number of handicaps.

Domestic instability; a weak military and economic complex; the philosophical inclinations of Jawaharlal Nehru; territorial interests in Kashmir, Goa, and on the border with China; India's colonial experience; and the tug and pull of the superpowers under the cold war: All these factors influenced Indian foreign policy to a greater or lesser extent. One fact, however, is apparent. The shape of Indian foreign policy in its final analysis was the work of Nehru alone until he died.

Naturally, like the executive head of any other state Nehru received counsel and information from most of the traditional sources. Evidence indicates that he discussed foreign policy matters with select members of his cabinet, and consulted the intelligence channels within the country and abroad, even though these channels were never adequate. But as both prime minister and president of the ruling Indian National Congress Party, there were few restraints upon him. In the parliament his party enjoyed a near two-third majority. He had the unquestioned support of the Indian masses. While scattered opposition in the parliament and some national newspapers continually criticized his policies, at times with a certain vehemence, his only real constraints were pressing domestic interests, a weak military and economic capability, and American and Soviet interests in Asia and elsewhere. Nonetheless, during independent India's formative years, her domestic and international policy reflected in the main Nehru's judgment as to the country's needs and her proper role in world affairs.

It must be emphasized that Nehru was not a dictator by temperament. Nor have the formal institutions of constitutional government been absent in India. A combination of factors led to the situation which permitted Nehru maximum flexibility in policy making. Among the leaders of the successful nationalist movement, Mahatma Gandhi and Sardar Vallabhbhai Patel were the only men besides Nehru who had both the national mass support and the respect of their peer group needed to challenge Nehru's ideas. With their death soon after India's independence, Nehru was left alone to share the burdens and the glory of independence.

There is no evidence that he suppressed challenges to his leadership. Actually, individuals with nationwide political support, trust of the masses, and the intellectual depth characteristic of Nehru were not flooding the political marketplace. Bureaucratic genius was there, in the Indian civil service and the Indian army. But it had been born and nourished under British control. It was not in touch with the Indian masses; it did not embrace popular feelings; and it was hardly a creative force. Political parties other than the Indian National Congress lacked the national base as well as the talent which might have produced the alternative to Nehru's leadership. Some of these factors are the natural consequences of prolonged foreign rule. Apparently, Nehru's domination of the Indian scene was not entirely of his own making.

India did not present a very promising picture in the aftermath of independence. Partition of the subcontinent into India and Pakistan in 1947 gave rise to mass migration on both sides, frustration, bitterness, and riots of an unprecedented violent nature, and a military engagement in Kashmir. Division of military and industrial resources, both in terms of men and materials, between the two independent states of India and Pakistan meant that the meager capabilities were further strained in attempts to stabilize the home front. Even though India had achieved comparative stability at home by 1950, for the last twenty-five years her economic and military resources have been for the most part devoted toward maintaining internal stability.

Logically, India's leadership should have concentrated its attention on the domestic scene and left the international stage to be managed by major powers, mainly the United States and the Soviet Union. But this is exactly what disturbed Nehru most. Firstly, he was convinced that cold war tensions between the two major powers not only threatened world peace, but affected the interests of every state, large and small. Secondly, he could not tolerate the thought that the future of the world was to be decided alone by the two most powerful nations of the world. And inasmuch as he thought of India in terms of her past glory and unmatched spiritual heritage, there was no question in his mind that India had to play a positive role in world politics.

Thus, without the necessary military and economic ability, India plunged into international politics, justifying her actions in the name of morality and world peace. Nehru sought to lead the Asian states away from alliances with the Western or Eastern bloc of nations, and at the same time he attempted to exert influence on the policies of the U.S.A. and USSR, all in the name of prevention of a third world war and the principle of self-determination. He did not hesitate to request and receive economic assistance from America and Russia, but when these nations attempted to tie strings to the aid, Nehru protested that it was the moral obligation of rich and powerful states to come to the rescue of the poor. What is interesting is that vagaries of international events for a brief period seemed to indicate that India was achieving her objectives successfully. But it was not long before the deteriorating economic situation in India, military engagements in Kashmir, Goa and the Himalayan border, and certain changes on the international scene proved the impossibility of success of her experiment in nonalignment. Reality finally pressed itself upon the Indian foreign policymakers. But old habits and patterns of thought die hard. It took three wars before major changes emerged in the fundamentals of Indian foreign policy.

In the process of evolution, India's foreign policy passed through three distinct periods of development. During the first period, roughly from 1947 to 1962, India's policy abroad was marked by nonalignment, idealism, and active internationalism. Nonalignment, a foreign policy feature markedly different from the guaranteed neutrality of Austria, or the traditional neutrality of Switzerland, or the neutrality of a nonbelligerent in a war, held special significance in the post-World War II period. A distinctive trait of the newly independent states of Asia and Africa, it emerged as an approach to the intense antagonism that had developed between the United States and the Soviet Union soon after 1945. For India it meant that she would not be drawn into any alliance which was either anti-U.S. or anti-USSR.

Nonalignment, however, was hardly adequate as a sole response to the dominant international force at the time of Indian independence. India's leaders, in order to arouse the masses to national consciousness, had repeatedly fed them the message of India's past humanism and spiritual greatness.[1] Apparently Indian foreign policymakers became convinced that their country must carry this crusading spirit into world politics. Therefore, it was in character for India to weld idealism with nonalignment. Her idealism was expressed in the high moral tone of Prime Minister Nehru's statements before the bar of world opinion. It was manifest in India's actions in the United Nations. Indian idealism appeared in Nehru's exhortations to the states of Asia and Africa to pursue an independent course in foreign policy and to keep their respective continents free from European interference. Undoubtedly, convinced of her high moral commitment in foreign policy matters, India felt safe in taking the Kashmir issue to the United Nations in 1948, at a time when she felt certain she had a military victory at hand.

The Korean conflict thrust India onto the international stage. As the first open confrontation between the forces representing communism and anticommunism, Korean fighting threatened to engulf the whole of Asia and possibly the world in a total war. India was concerned. Also, as an Asian power she wished to be consulted whenever the future of any part of Asia was being debated. With little military strength to back her, India could not do much to directly influence the course of events in Korea. However, armed with a nonaligned posture and appeals for peace, she could plead with Moscow and Washington to make every effort to confine the hostilities to Korea and undertake negotiations for a peaceful settlement. India vigorously pursued this course in the United Nations and outside it. At first her efforts failed, but new developments in the situation worked to favor her position. As a part of the settlement of the Korean question, India emerged as the Chairman of the Neutral Nations Repatriation Commission which handled the thorny problem of exchange of prisoners.

Prime Minister Nehru and his advisers saw the outcome as testimony that they had succeeded in striking a modus vivendi with the new regime in neighboring China,[2] even though the new masters of that country displayed great pride in their communist affiliation. Indian leadership found in this experience a confirmation that the nonalignment approach not only permitted flexibility in the international arena, but also enabled India to secure a position of world leadership. Above all, as a consequence of the events in Korea, India's foreign policymakers apparently came to believe that India's credentials as an international mediator had been established. India's U.N. representative Krishna Menon remarked at a news conference in New Delhi in May 1955: "The purpose of people like us, who are neither mediators nor busybodies, is that we allow ourselves to be utilized—or we utilize ourselves—in order to contribute towards harmony. This is part of our domestic and foreign outlook."[3]

However, despite her role as a mediator, her posture of nonalignment, and her efforts to lead the Afro-Asian states toward neutralism, India was unable to prevent South and Southeast Asia from being engulfed in major power rivalries. In 1954 the United States and Pakistan concluded a military pact. In 1955, the South East Asia Treaty, aimed at the communist countries, went into effect, and in the same year Pakistan became a member of the Baghdad pact (CENTO after 1959), which was designed to stop communist expansion in the Middle East.

During the same period, India moved closer to China and the Soviet Union. India signed the famous Panch Sheel treaty of friendship with China in 1954. During Khrushchev's and Bulganin's visit in 1955, India and the USSR concluded a major trade pact. Also for the first time, Moscow openly declared her support for India's position in Kashmir and Goa. Thus even if India had achieved some success as an international mediator, she had failed in her attempts to keep Asia free from cold war politics.

Admittedly, this was because the major powers had no intention of abandoning their influence and interests in Asia. But it was also an indication that India's occupation with building herself as a world leader and mediator was of little consequence in helping her solve problems closer to home.

India's foreign policy began to experience pressures in late 1956. The Suez crisis and the Hungarian crisis erupted in the fall of that year. India was quick to condemn Britain and France when they attacked Egypt. But soon after, when the Russian forces moved into Hungary and crushed the revolt against Soviet occupation, India did not immediately censure the USSR for her action. Response to India's conduct was sharp. Her claims to high moral standards and her posture of nonalignment were severely compromised.

As a state that never failed to condemn the use of force on the international scene, India's position became untenable when her troops crossed into Goa in 1961 and expelled the Portuguese. Even if the action appeared justified to India's policymakers, it was a difficult position to uphold for a state that repeatedly invoked peace and morality as the cardinal principles of her foreign policy.

It was in 1959, in the aftermath of the Tibetan revolt against Chinese occupation, that cracks began to appear in India's foreign policy. The Dalai Lama, ruler of Tibet, fled and took refuge in India. When India refused to surrender him to the Chinese government, China proceeded to put pressure on India's northern borders. Troops clashed and relations between India and China deteriorated steadily.

India's foreign policy was forced to change direction when the People's Republic of China mounted a large-scale attack against her in 1962. Military aid speedily dispatched by Britain and the United States enabled India to hold the Chinese after suffering a series of reverses. Addressing a conference of provincial governors on October 25, Prime Minister Nehru said that China's "massive invasion" had made India realize that she had been "out of touch with reality," and had shocked India out of the "artificial atmosphere of our own creation."

The post-1962 period was generally marked by India's sense of rejection and isolation; her pretensions of global power came to an end. Even her role as a regional power was in doubt. India's policymakers did not recognize until 1962, when humiliation at the hands of the Chinese brought them closer to the realities of national interest and power politics, that their assumption of unquestioned leadership in the Asian world was completely false. The response of the other Asian states to the Sino-Indian conflict was somewhat akin to the Indian response to Soviet-American hostility.

Aside from the influence of Buddhism and some aspects of Hinduism on Southeast Asian and East Asian peoples, their history, politics, and culture bear little resemblance to India's. Common colonial experience which evoked mutual expressions of sympathy in support of national independence movements proved to be a temporary bond. Even as India's independence provided encouragement and support for self-determination demands in other parts of Asia, each nation state after achieving freedom pursued a policy pattern reflecting the will of its own power elites. The military and economic interests of the small states of Asia often clashed and only rarely coincided with those of India.

It appears that Indian leadership simply failed to perceive some of these facts prior to the clash with China. Nehru was shocked and disappointed at the reaction of the Afro-Asian World to the developments in the Sino-Indian relationship. But India could now see that her relations with the Third World too had to be readjusted.

And so in the aftermath of 1962 began the second phase of Indian foreign policy which lasted roughly until 1971. After 1962, India's arena of action became severly limited. Nehru died in 1964.[4] His successors ceased to condemn or commend activities of world powers; they sought no role for India either as a mediator or pacesetter. For the first time they recognized that India's security was in real danger. If until then Pakistan alone stood as the enemy, China had now joined her. Would there be an alliance between China and Pakistan? Despite her anticommunist security pact with the United States, would Pakistan turn to China and with some assurance from her proceed to annex Kashmir? The possibility loomed large, especially since even during the heyday of Sino-Indian friendship, China, unlike Russia, had maintained a scrupulous neutrality on the Kashmir issue.

Without admitting that he was compromising his stance of nonalignment, Nehru turned toward the United States, Great Britain, and the Soviet Union for military assistance to bolster India's defenses. This could have been a turning point in Indo-American relations. If India did not become heavily dependent upon the U.S. for military aid, it is because in deference to Pakistan's wishes America refused to give India supersonic aircraft, air-to-air missiles, and heavy tanks. India came to realize that the benefits of nonalignment were strictly limited: It had failed to provide national security and offered no guarantee for necessary military and economic assistance.

Nineteen sixty-five saw India involved in the short-lived

Indo-Pak war, brought to a halt by combined Soviet-American pressure. China did not intervene, for she was warned by the United States that such an action would result in serious consequences. At the initiative of the Soviet Union, India and Pakistan worked out the Tashkent Agreement. But the settlement at Tashkent neither resolved the outstanding issues between the two countries, nor did it bring the subcontinent closer to permanent peace.

The sudden death of India's second prime minister, L. B. Shastri, at the end of the Tashkent Conference in January, 1966, brought new leadership to power in New Delhi. During the first few years of her rule, the new prime minister Mrs. Indira Gandhi was mostly occupied with consolidating her power on the homefront. She found little opportunity to do much in the area of India's foreign policy which had been dominated by the 1962 and 1965 wars.

Events on the subcontinent in 1971 permitted Mrs. Gandhi to give a shape and direction to Indian foreign policy which was not only distinct from earlier periods, but which will probably remain India's guide for a long time to come.

In March, 1971, political developments in East and West Pakistan culminated in a civil war. As a result nearly 10 million refugees from East Pakistan fled to the neighboring state of West Bengal in India, creating an untenable economic problem for India. At the same time, the brutal suppression of the Bengalis in East Pakistan generated a tremendous pressure for recognition of the free government of Bangladesh and intervention by the Indian army.

India's leaders took two highly significant steps at this time which broke with her past patterns of behavior in international politics. On August 9, 1971, India and the USSR signed a treaty of peace and friendship which pledged: "In the event of either party being subjected to an attack or a threat thereof, the High Contracting Parties shall immediately enter into mutual consultations in order to remove such threat and to take appropriate effective measures to ensure peace and the security of their countries."[5]

Second, in the early hours of December 4, 1971, after a preemptive airstrike by the Pakistani Air Force on a number of Indian airfields, India declared war on Pakistan. Indian troops moved into East Pakistan with full force. When the 14 day confrontation was over the face of the subcontinent had changed and so had the direction and content of Indian foreign policy.

This third Indo-Pak war ended in a severe defeat for Pakistan. The country was divided. East Pakistan emerged as the independent state of Bangladesh. India was now the dominant power on the subcontinent of South Asia. But Pakistan's defeat and the subsequent birth of Bangladesh could not have occurred without the agreement which promised India full support of the Soviet Union.

The treaty has long-range ramifications for Indian foreign policy since it obligates the two parties not to take any action which would jeopardize the interests of the other party.

Had India not exploded a nuclear device in 1974, it would have been easy to maintain that the new course of foreign policy selected by Mrs. Gandhi meant very close ties with the Soviet Union, especially in the face of Sino-American detente and Washington's continuing friendship with Pakistan.

However, the emergence of India as the sixth nuclear power, a visit to India by Secretary of State Henry Kissinger during October, 1974, and some of India's overtures toward the U.S., leave room to believe that Mrs. Gandhi desires to leave her options open, and India's current foreign policy has greater flexibility than has been assumed.

India's nuclear capability has added strength to Mrs. Gandhi's repeated statements that the Indo-Soviet treaty does not strap her nation's foreign policy. Future Sino-Indian and Indo-American relations will reveal the true character of the situation. Yet it is evident that by 1972 India had opened a new chapter in her foreign policy, marked by pragmatism, a sense of new confidence and a measure of self-reliance, possibly exaggerated, which had never prevailed before. India no longer seeks a global role, and the superpowers no longer solicit her mediation as they did in the days of the cold war. India appears to have reconciled to the fact that she has not been effective in creating a united front of Third World countries. Experience in three wars has made her highly security conscious, and she has at last become convinced that her security must be built on a foundation other than the international goodwill that she chased for more than two decades.

The following pages focus attention on India's capabilities, and the shape and process of her foreign policy formulation today and in the future. The topics dealt with are in response to a set of theses projected in the core volume of this series,[6] for example, that a nation's role on the world scene over a period of time is in a major way a reflection of its capabilities. Further, in this view, not only is the standing of a given state among the world states measured by the capability factor, it also plays a decisive part in determining the long-range prospects of success or failure of a state's foreign policy. While material resources alone do not constitute the total capability of a state, "a State's position in the international power structure . . . is the strongest environmental or international-systemic influence on state behavior."[7] The chapter on India's capabilities attempts to probe how this factor has affected her foreign policy.

The author of the core volume adopts the hypothesis that the nature of a country's political leadership heavily influences its foreign policy. He holds that when a state has a strong-willed leadership, its policy more or less mirrors the world perceptions of the leadership. On the other hand, when will and determination are lacking, such factors as history, traditions, and stable bureaucratic habit tend to mold the shape of foreign policy. The chapters dealing with Indian political beliefs, and the formulation process of India's foreign policy, examine the character and the role of Indian leadership with a view to assess whether India's policy has been dominated by individual preferences or her cultural background and historical traditions.

Similarly, it is postulated that the influence of political institutions, political culture, or the style of the domestic political process on foreign policy might be secondary. But these factors assume considerable significance and explain individual policies when the leadership is not strong willed, and the capability aspect does not in itself account for the foreign policy posture. Accordingly, this study examines India's Parliament and the political process to assess the impact they have had on India's international dealings.

On June 26, 1975, the president of India declared a nationwide state of emergency. As a result, all power came to rest in the hands of Prime Minister Gandhi. The government has imposed press censorship. Civil liberties have been suspended. Many members of the opposition have been arrested, and extremist religious and political parties have been banned. While this influences the functions of the political institutions and the political process, its impact on foreign policy appears negligible. Furthermore, since the input of the parliament and the press in foreign policy making has been minimal, as the following pages indicate, the foreign policy formulation process and the orientation of India's foreign policy remain unaffected by the recent events. India's foreign relations provide us with one case study in a series designed to introduce the student to a comparative analysis of foreign policies and foreign policy making.

Notes

[1] In this, Indian leadership was approved not only by many Western scholars, but also by such historical evidence as Emperor Ashoka's becoming a Buddhist and abandoning his imperial ambitions at the height of his power. Writings of such men as Bertrand Russell, Norman Cousins and Arne Naess merit attention in this regard.

[2] Whenever China is mentioned the reference is to People's Republic of China, unless otherwise indicated.

[3] *The Hindu* (Madras), May 31, 1955.

[4] Nehru's successor, Prime Minister Shastri, headed the government

for a very short time; he died in January, 1966. Shastri was followed by the present prime minister of India, Mrs. Indira Gandhi.

⁵N. M. Ghatate, ed., *Indo-Soviet Treaty* (New Delhi: Deendayal Research Institute, 1972), p. 15.

⁶Wilkinson, *Comparative Foreign Relations: Framework and Methods*

⁷Ibid., p. 27.

2

India's Capability Factor and Foreign Policy

If the twentieth century is marked by the birth of the League of Nations and the United Nations, agencies which were created in the hope of curbing international conflict and providing peaceful settlement of international disputes, it is also the century marked by two world wars, many small wars, and the ever-present threat of a third world war. Given the nature of the international state system, war continues to be an essential instrument of foreign policy. As Raymond Aron has said: "Rationality, in fact, dictates reflection on peace despite the uproar of the melee, and on war when weapons are silent. The commerce of nations is continuous; diplomacy and war are only complementary modalities, one or the other dominating in turn, without one ever entirely giving way to the other except in the extreme case either of absolute hostility, or of absolute friendship or total federation."[1]

As long as sovereign states continue to organize and accumulate massive means of violence with no positive control from any source, war will remain the final arbiter of quarrels among nation states, and military power will remain an important and active instrument of foreign policy. However, wars differ in character and intensity. Their nature is dictated both by the capacity of states to make war, and their defense and foreign policies. Thus even as every state maintains a military machine, its total strength and its state of readiness varies, dependent upon its philosophical approach to war as a positive or a negative instrument of policy, its estimate of the size and source of threat to its sovereign status, and the content and character of its physical resources.[2]

India's leaders have always denounced war as an instrument of foreign policy. However, it is true that Gandhi alone stood against any form of organized military machine after India became independent. As the first prime minister of independent India, Nehru put together a military force for security purposes. But being antimilitary in spirit, he deemphasized India's defense needs. The task of building an effective military machine was left to Lal Bahadur Shastri, and more so to Mrs. Indira Gandhi, the two who followed Nehru in the office of the prime minister. Nehru's reluctance to rely on military force can be partly attributed to his philosophical orientation, and partly to his belief that there was no major threat to India's security. But by the time Shastri and later Mrs. Gandhi came to power, the character of military threats from bordering states was ominous enough so that political reality left them with no choice other than rapid military buildup.

Prime Minister Nehru's statements before and during the early period of India's independence suggest that he did not consider it necessary for India to adopt a major program of armament. He felt India should maintain a small military force, sufficient to provide internal stability and viable defense against any external threat to Indian security, which he perceived as being minimal. As one writer has stated:

> By the eve of the Second World War, therefore, the framework of Indian defence policy had been defined by the man whose predispositions were to be mirrored in the defense posture ultimately adopted by the Indian Union. Nehru envisaged a free India secure against attack either by its geo-strategic position, its size, or the balance of power. He did not dismiss the possibility of aggressive actions against India by Afghanistan or the tribes on the North-West Frontier, but he was inclined to minimize these threats as mostly of nuisance value and containable by relatively small but efficient armed forces.[3]

Krishna Menon, India's Defense Minister from 1957 to 1962, said in an interview in 1964: "Our defense policy until the Chinese invaded us was intended to resist an attack from Pakistan . . . it is also quite true that considering the size of our country we have a small army."[4]

Nehru himself lends weight to these observations, for speaking before the Indian Constituent Assembly in March, 1948, he said:

> We are not citizens of a weak or mean country and I think it is foolish for us to get frightened, even from a military point of view, of the greatest of the powers today ... after all in the past, as a national movement, we opposed one of the greatest of World Powers. We opposed it in a particular way and in a large measure succeeded in that way, and I have no doubt that if the worst comes to the worst—and in a military sense we cannot meet these great Powers—it is far better for us to fight in our own way (through nonviolence) than submit to them and lose all the ideals we have.[5]

On another occasion Nehru reiterated the same thoughts: "We hear a lot about the atom bomb and the various kinds of energy that it represents and in essence today there is a conflict in the world between two things, the atom bomb and what it represents and the spirit of humanity. I hope that while India will no doubt play a great part in all the national spheres, she will always lay stress on the spirit of humanity and I have no doubt in my mind that ultimately in this conflict that is confronting the world the human spirit will prevail over the atom bomb."[6]

Examining other statements of Nehru, one becomes aware that as prime minister and external affairs minister, he fully recognized the need for a military establishment in independent India. While it did not appeal to him, he certainly understood the game of power politics in international affairs. On the other hand he had no intention of giving priority to building India into a militarily strong state. Possibly his idealism led him to believe that because of her ancient spiritual heritage India had to play a role distinctly different from other nation states. He felt a compulsion to stress moral force as an active instrument for realizing world peace.

Commenting on the defense aspect of India's policies, Lt. General B. M. Kaul, at one time Chief of the General Staff of the Indian Army, has written:

> Ever since independence, most of our leaders believed that we attained freedom through nonviolence and therefore thought that if we could expel a power like the British without the use of arms and nonviolently, there was little point in wasting large—even though essential—expenditure on our armed forces.... Even after the emergence and discovery of the Chinese build-up along our borders ... government continued to be apathetic.... Consequently, the Armed Forces did not receive the attention they deserved, remained inadequate in shape and size ... and hence unprepared for war, mainly because of the mental attitude of our government towards this problem.[7]

The same viewpoint is confirmed by a statement of onetime Secretary of Defense H. M. Patel, who said in late 1962: "Were it not for our strained relations with Pakistan ever since Independence, we might well have adopted the rather tempting policy of more or less total disarmament."[8]

Nehru deemphasized the role of armed strength on ideological grounds; but as pointed out earlier he was confirmed in this view by his perceptions of the size and the source of threat to Indian security. At the time of independence and up to the day of confrontation with the Chinese in 1962, Prime Minister Nehru was convinced that there was virtually no serious threat to India's security from any external source.

The first Indo-Pak clash over Kashmir took place in October, 1947. While a cease-fire arranged by the United Nations prevailed from 1949 onward, no permanent settlement was worked out. The possibility of renewed conflict between the two neighbors remained alive, but Nehru was convinced that the parties to the conflict would in the end work out a solution peacefully.

Similarly, when China occupied Tibet in 1950, not only did India discourage the United Nations from taking up the Tibetan question, despite earlier protestations, but in continuing to push for UN recognition of the People's Republic of China, India sought to demonstrate that she was not apprehensive about Chinese expansionism. This self-assurance permitted Nehru to say to the Indian Parliament in February, 1953: "I am confident that today there is no country which is actually hostile to us. Naturally, some countries are more friendly than others but those who are occasionally critical of us do not harbor any permanent resentment against us."[9]

Even after the signing of the U.S.-Pak security pact in 1954, which India interpreted as being anti-Indian because it strengthened Pakistan militarily, Nehru insisted on assuring the Soviets on his visit to the Kremlin in 1955 that "we have no enemies."[10] During this visit Nehru was seeking, and did receive, Soviet assistance in the Security Council to block any moves that could be detrimental to Indian interests in Kashmir. But Nehru had no intentions of asking for military aid, for according to his readings no contingency existed that required such an arrangement.

In 1959 it became clear that India and China had a strong disagreement as to their exact common boundary, and border clashes had taken place between army patrols from both sides. One author comments:

> "Yet ... Nehru seemed to believe that the Chinese had no hostile intentions against India, and that even if they had aggressive intentions, these could be thwarted by gestures of friendship on India's part. ... Nehru's apparently idealistic assessment of Chinese motives was also perhaps responsible for his regarding the incursions across India's borders as 'petty disputes' over land where 'not a blade of grass grows,' and for keeping the Indian parliament and people ignorant of Chinese penetration into Ladakh for one year after the Aksai Chin road was completed by the Chinese. Not until it was too late did Nehru start talking of things which were in the shade having come into the light, of

the Chinese valuing India's friendship to a low extent, of Chinese betrayal; and confessing that he had not in fact considered any aggression by China likely and that a grave mistake had been made."[11]

K. P. S. Menon has written that in the first decade of her independence, "... India had a rosy view of the world. That was because independence came to her more easily than to other countries under the imperialist yoke. When India attained independence in a civilized nonviolent way, the whole world seemed to welcome it; and India fondly hoped that she could bask forever in the sunshine of universal friendship."[12]

Indian leadership attitudes until mid-1960 were not conducive to building a strong military power. By 1966, however, in the aftermath of the Indo-Pak war, there could be no doubt that India now had two active sources of threat, China and Pakistan. Both these countries held territorial claims against India. Both had displayed their willingness to use force to realize their objectives. There was no guarantee that the forces which had constrained them from achieving complete victory over India in the past would work in the future. And if India desired to meet this challenge, she had no choice but to build a more formidable and effective military machine. It was under these pressures that India started on the road to a military buildup which, as a measure of her improved power position, enabled her to fight a decisive war against Pakistan in December, 1971. These pressures also led India to sign a security pact with Russia in August, 1971 which put a severe check on Chinese ability to coerce India. To cap it all, India exploded a nuclear device in 1974. This made it manifest that India's defense posture and capability had turned full circle.

India's Military Capability

During World War II, at its peak, the Indian army had reached a strength of two million men, and was led almost exclusively by more than eight thousand British officers. However, gradual demobilization was started as early as 1944. By 1946, as it became clear that India was to be granted independence, the process of demobilization was well on its way. In September, 1946, the Ayyangar Committee was appointed to tackle the problem of peacetime strength and nationalization of the armed forces. Before the Committee had completed its task, the British government announced its decision to partition the Indian subcontinent into the two separate nations of India and Pakistan. Thus after August, 1947, the question was not merely one of nationalization or Indianization, the armed forces had to be divided between India and Pakistan on a mutually acceptable basis. And the division of the armed forces meant not only partitioning of men, equipment, and facilities, it also "... necessitated the giving of option to every Muslim soldier, sailor and airman resident in the areas which constituted India after partition, and every Hindu soldier, sailor and airman resident in areas which formed Pakistan, to remain with the Indian armed forces or to join Pakistan armed forces, and vice versa."[13]

Thus at the time of independence in August, 1947, planning for a peacetime armed forces hit a snag. Furthermore, while the prime minister and the defense minister repeatedly talked of additional reductions in the armed forces because of financial reasons, events beyond their control continued to dictate a larger Indian armed force, though the size was never formidable.

Even as free India began the task of organizing her military capability under most unfavorable conditions, she called upon her armies to man several fronts at the dawn of independence. As a result of mutual fear, hatred, and mass killings in the wake of partition, as many as eight to ten million people fled across the borders in both directions between India and Pakistan, leaving behind their homes, belongings, and even family members. These unsettled conditions had to be managed by the army.

Indian and Pakistani armies battled each other over territorial claims in Kashmir from September, 1947 to January, 1949, when the United Nations succeeded in effecting a cease-fire. Other dislocations directly associated with partition were the upheavals in the princely states of Junagadh and Hyderabad. Reliance upon the army for handling all these situations appears to have discouraged plans for any cutbacks immediately after independence. And when in 1949 these problems seemed under control, a series of insurrections within India by the Communists, as well as the victory of the Chinese Communists on mainland China, prevented any reductions seen fit by the administration as economy measures.[14]

On Independence Day, India had at her disposal a mere skeleton of some 150 officers and 576 noncommissioned officers, both civil and military, with a total of 280,000 armed forces personnel of all categories. Her Navy and Air Force were so insignificant that they could hardly be considered as separate services. While the picture did change between 1947 and 1959 in regard to the number of officers, as well as the size of the Navy and the Air Force, the total strength of the military forces hovered around 300,000 during these years. Speaking before the Indian Parliament in March, 1949, India's first defense minister, Sardar Baldev Singh, reviewed certain features of organization and composition of the Indian military. He stated that independent India, following democratic practice, had placed the military under tight civilian control. Indianization of the officer corps had proceeded rapidly so that only a handful of British officers remained by 1949; after a few more years they too left the Indian service.[15] Independent India created three separate Services Headquarters, each under its own Chief of Staff and Commander-in-Chief, to permit the Navy and Air Force to expand on their own without being overshadowed by the larger Army.

Until independence, India was almost wholly dependent on facilities in Great Britain for higher and intensive training of her armed forces. The few training institutions which did exist on Indian soil were so situated that on partition those with any merit were inherited by Pakistan. The defense minister announced intentions to establish a new National Academy, the School of Military Engineering, the Armed Forces Medical College, the Defense Science Organization, and Air Force and Naval Technical Schools, as fast as resources permitted.

Speaking of ordnance factories, the defense minister pointed out that India lacked the equipment, the resources, and the technical staff for self-sufficiency. He stated that while a few factories for production of small arms did exist in India, and there was intention of adding a few more, India had to depend upon foreign sources for modern and heavy firepower.[16]

The picture of India's military strength as it stood during the period between independence day and the Chinese attack in 1962 reveals two facts: Independent India's policymakers had assessed the international situation, and their country's financial resources and demands, and thus sought to create a small defense force which could be possibly expanded with speed in a crisis. Secondly, they were prepared to depend upon foreign sources for major supplies of heavy armament for many years to come.[17]

Thus on the eve of the large scale attack by China against India on October 20, 1962, India was ill-equipped, and found her undersized army unable to meet the challenge from across the Himalayan borders.

The outdated equipment supplied to these forces was a major handicap. As recently as 1962, the Indian army lacked a good rifle, and was using a local version of the World War I bolt-action .303 British Enfield. The range of the Indian Army's locally produced mortars was very limited—only 4,700 yards as compared to the 7,900 yard range of a similar U.S.-produced weapon. India had supplied her armored units with some 30 U.S. Sherman tanks, about 200 British Centurion heavy tanks, and early 150 French AMX light tanks; but there was no indigenous tank production until this period. Aside from securing a very limited supply of jeeps from the British in 1950-51, the Indian army depended mostly upon some 20,000 overhauled trucks of all types left from the World War II stocks.[18]

The Indian army's need for new equipment in 1962 was desperate. The following quotation from Welles Hangen is quite revealing:

> When Indian troops overran Goa in December 1961, many marched in canvas shoes because a contract for boots had been switched from the Bata Company to a small Indian firm, which failed to deliver.
>
> While the old Ishapore rifle factory near Calcutta is still unable to make a modern rifle, it did turn out, between 1958 and 1960, a total of fifteen espresso coffee machines at a cost of 4,500 rupees (about $900) apiece. None of these not-so-violent weapons could be sold to the public....
>
> Armed with espresso coffee machines and canvas shoes, even the finest Indian troops are ill-equipped to guard the country's 8,200 miles of land frontier and 3,500 miles of sea frontier.[19]

India's ground forces were supported by a small air force that relied almost exclusively on aircraft and related equipment from Britain, France, Russia, and the United States. It had no effective ground radar net for strategic assistance.

In 1962 the Indian Navy was incapable of any more than a limited defensive mission. Vice-Admiral Parry of the Indian navy stated at a press conference in January, 1950, that the Navy planned to develop a small task force consisting of one light fleet carrier, three light cruisers, eight to nine destroyers, and the requisite support vessels.[20] A decade later the size of the Indian Navy had come close to this dimension but did not quite reach the mark because of financial difficulties. India had no submarine of her own and continued to depend upon periodic visits by British submarines for training in antisubmarine warfare.

The Chinese offensive all along India's northern borders lasted from October 20 to November 21, 1962, when the Chinese declared a unilateral cease-fire and withdrew voluntarily from many of the forward positions. The manner in which the Indian army was put to rout on almost every front shocked the politicians and the professionals alike. Suddenly the policymakers at all levels became aware of the sad state of India's military capabilities.

Soon after the clash with the Chinese, Indian arms missions were dispatched to the United States, Great Britain, the Soviet Union, and several Commonwealth countries to finalize negotiations regarding long term military requirements. In 1964 the Indian government disclosed a Five Year Defense Plan to meet the Chinese threat. The Plan, covering the period from April, 1964 to March, 1969, expressed India's resolve to create a modern land force of 825,000 men, a 45 squadron air force with the latest radar and communication facilities, and a modernized navy. The Plan also conceived the establishment of an adequate network of border roads and supply lines, as well as a base for indigenous production of defense equipment to meet most requirements of the armed forces.

Even before the first phase of this new attempt to increase the country's military strength had been fully realized, India was confronted with another test of her military capability. The long-standing dispute between India and Pakistan over Kashmir erupted into a major confrontation between the armed forces of the two countries.

On August 5, 1965, a force of about 5,000 infiltrators under the command of a Pakistani general crossed the border into the Indian part of Jammu and Kashmir, after India announced she would assume administration of the entire state. They committed many acts of sabotage, but India's Security Forces did succeed in chasing them back into Pakistani territory. This led to the involvement of regular Pakistani forces in September. In an attempt to divert the attention of Pakistan from the Jammu and Kashmir theater, the Indian military opened up a front along the West Punjab border of Pakistan. While the Indian army struck a limited number of successful blows against the Pakistani army, especially in the area of tank battles, and made some inroads into Pakistan's territory, the confrontation was in no way decisive, and it is questionable whether the armed forces of either country had the capacity to fight to a decisive end. The United States, the Soviet Union, and Britain were quick to apply pressure on both India and Pakistan to cease hostilities. When the United States and Great Britain announced the suspension of military as well as economic aid to both the belligerents until normalization of the situation, India and Pakistan accepted the United Nations' sponsored cease-fire on September 23, even as both complained bitterly of having been let down by the Western powers.

For India this "limited war" of 1965, coming on the heels of the 1962 experience, had great significance. The antimilitary tradition began to give way to a recognition of the fact that the military was an essential component of the state. India was, more than ever before, awakened to the realization that heavy reliance upon other powers for modern military equipment was a constraint upon her policy. Above all it became clear to India that notwithstanding earlier attitudes and estimates, she had to prepare in the future for a possible two-pronged military threat from China and Pakistan.

Between 1966 and 1971, India's armed strength increased dramatically. By 1971 defense spending had climbed to an all-time high of 20% of the total annual budget. While India remained dependent upon foreign sources for heavy fire power, she was producing large quantities of trucks, small arms, light artillery, and tanks locally.[21] New training techniques were introduced to prepare the army for infiltration, guerrilla warfare and encounter at high altitudes. The Indian army was reorganized. The term of active duty for servicemen was increased, and improved benefits raised the morale of the careerists. On the eve of India's major confrontation with Pakistan in December, 1971, the state of India's military preparedness was very different from what it had been in 1962 or 1965.

When the 14 day war began, the relative size of the armed forces of the belligerents was quite disproportionate. India's armed forces stood at 850,000 as opposed to Pakistan's total of 392,000. India's armored divisions had close to 1500 tanks at their disposal as opposed to Pakistan's 900. While Pakistan relied mostly on Patton and Sherman tanks supplied by the U.S.A., India's tank force was made up of Vijayanta tanks of indigenous production, Soviet-made T-54 and T-55 tanks, Centurion Tanks and some light armor tanks. India's Naval Force consisted of 40,000 men as opposed to Pakistan's 10,000. India had one aircraft carrier, Pakistan had none. Pakistan's three submarines and 12 midget submarines were matched by India's four submarines (all acquired from the USSR), two cruisers, three destroyers, and five antisubmarine frigates. India's Air Force consisted of 90,000 men and 625 combat aircraft. Pakistan's Air Force was made up of 30,000 men and 285 combat aircraft. India's air fleet relied mainly on eight squadrons of MIG 21 fighter inceptors, eight squadrons of Gnats, six squadrons of Hunters and five squadrons of Sukhoi-7. Pakistan's air power rested mostly on eight squadrons of Sabre jets, close to two squadrons of French Mirages, five squadrons of MIG 19 fighter bombers, one squadron of F-104 Phantoms and one squadron of IL-28 bombers procured from China.[22]

India's armed might in 1971 was easily twice its 1965 size. Despite the prevalent myth in many quarters that Pakistan made up for her handicap in size by the superior fighting quality of her armed forces, Indian armies executed a swift and decisive victory over her opponents. This led the United States to express the fear that India was possibly on her way to capturing the whole of Pakistan, a fear which proved to be misplaced when India declared a unilateral ceasefire, after Pakistani armies had surrendered in East Pakistan. India's military did demonstrate that their fighting ability had improved considerably compared to their performance in 1962 and 1965.

The division of Pakistan, and emergence of East Pakistan as the separate and independent state of Bangladesh, pointed to the fact that India had now become the dominant power on the subcontinent of South Asia. Indian leaders were quick to note, however, that for India, China still remained a major threat. This not only provided the rationale for military preparedness on a continuing basis, but it also made it mandatory that India not reduce her military strength. Jagjivan Ram, India's defense minister, told the Lok Sabha (lower house of the Indian Parliament) on May 2, 1972: "There is no obvious abatement in the threat to our security. The continuing interest of some great powers in maintaining tension on the subcontinent is a matter of common knowledge. The rivalry among the great powers in the Indian Ocean has added a fresh dimension. The recent extension of the jurisdiction of the U.S. Seventh Fleet is a matter of some concern. I have noted the desire of the House to see that deficiencies in our navy, air force and army are remedied as quickly as possible. I propose to do my best in this regard within the constraints imposed by technology, the availability of finance and the imperative requirements of the war on want and poverty."[23]

The above statement truly reflects the basic change that has taken place in India's attitude concerning the level of military arsenal considered necessary to maintain national security. The fact is that there is a growing feeling in India that possession of nuclear weapons is the natural next step on the road to developing a military potential that will be an effective deterrent.

India's Nuclear Capability

The world was informed on May 19, 1974, that India had successfully detonated its first nuclear device. While the Indian people, by and large, were elated to learn that their country had gained entry into the exclusive nuclear club, by no means did the five other members of the club or the rest of the world receive the news with any comfort. Prime Minister Mrs. Gandhi and the then defense minister, Jagjivan Ram, hastened to assure the world that the relatively low yield underground test was carried out to explore the uses of nuclear energy for such peaceful purposes as excavation and mining. They said further that India not only opposed military uses of nuclear explosions, but had no intentions of producing nuclear weapons. Other Indian officials were quick to point out that India had not broken any international agreements in carrying out the test. She had abided by the 1963 Test Ban Treaty by not exploding the device in the atmosphere. Since she did not sign the Nonproliferation Treaty, the question of abrogating it did not arise. But these pronouncements did not bring an end to fears in many quarters that the nuclear proliferation problem had been aggravated seriously, and that India had possibly become a participant in an arms race with China.

China, however, did not show any major concern. France and Russia, too, were subdued in their comment. Britain was unhappy. The United States reacted with dismay and disappointment, even though Secretary of State Henry Kissinger did say that in his opinion the test had no adverse effect on the balance of power in South Asia. The Third World countries reflected mixed feelings. Those who appeared most outraged at the Indian show of possible nuclear weapons capability were Japan, Pakistan, and Canada.

Japan is the only nation that has suffered the ravages of a nuclear attack. Therefore, it is to be expected that she dreads the prospect of nuclear proliferation. The chief cabinet secretary of Japan stated that Japan was opposed to any such test by any nation for any purpose, and they regretted that India took the action she did. Both Houses of the Japanese Parliament adopted a resolution protesting the test.[24]

However, while Japan signed the 1968 nuclear Nonproliferation Treaty soon after it was presented to the world by the United States and the Soviet Union, the Japanese Parliament has still not ratified the Treaty. So far there is only a minority of Japanese leaders who advocate nuclear capability to gain international prestige and to enable Japan to conduct a more independent foreign policy. But this could change. As one of the Japanese diplomats explained it to Sam Jameson, the *Los Angeles Times* correspondent in Tokyo, if India but not Japan were to be seated in the United Nations Security Council, the Japanese would feel discriminated against and would seriously consider obtaining nuclear power. A defense official told the same correspondent: "The question for Japan now is whether to become the seventh nuclear power, and there isn't much pressure to do so. But if it becomes an issue of whether we are to become the fourteenth power or the fifteenth power, the pressure (at home) could be overwhelming. That's the danger of proliferation."[25]

Obviously then, Japan's aversion to nuclear power capability in the hands of several states is qualified. She does not rule out the possibility of such capability herself. So her expressed opposition resulted primarily from a fear that Indian action would spur further proliferation, a supposition challenged by India.

That Pakistan was the loudest in her protests over the Indian nuclear explosion is easy to understand. Coming only two years after the humiliating Pakistani defeat in the Indo-Pak war of 1971, the Indian nuclear test was a sensitive reminder for Pakistan that India was now beyond doubt the dominant power on the subcontinent of South Asia. Prime Minister Z. A. Bhutto, at a press conference in Lahore, on May 19, said:

> Testing a nuclear device denotes that a country has acquired a nuclear weapon capability. But a nuclear weapon is not like conventional military weapons. It is primarily an instrument of pressure and coercion against nonnuclear powers.... We are determined not to be intimidated by this threat. I give a pledge to my countrymen that we will never let Pakistan be a victim of nuclear blackmail.... We will not

compromise the right of self-determination of the people of Jammu and Kashmir, nor will we accept Indian hegemony or domination over the subcontinent.[26]

To allay the fears of Pakistan, Prime Minister Gandhi sent a personal letter to Premier Bhutto through the Swiss Embassy in New Delhi on May 22. She assured him that India had no "hegemonistic" designs. She also stressed that India planned to use the nuclear energy for peaceful purposes only. She reiterated India's desire to resolve the differences between their two countries through peaceful bilateral negotiations without resort to the threat or use of force, as agreed upon in the Simla Agreement signed by both subsequent to the 1971 war.[27]

Since 1947, mutual distrust marks Indo-Pak relations. Any development which might enhance the industrial or military potential of India is bound to cause concern, fear, and indignation in the official circles of Pakistan. The case would be the same if the winds were blowing in the opposite direction. The fact is Pakistan remains secure in her dealings with India because the U.S.-Pakistan security treaty of 1954 is still in force.

Canada supplied the technology and the material that enabled India to start a nuclear energy program. Canada holds the opinion that in exploding a nuclear device India has betrayed her trust, accusing India of diverting resources from the initial grant for purposes which were excluded in the original agreement. This agreement laid the groundwork for cooperation between the two countries for nuclear energy development in India.

The Canadian External Affairs Minister, Mr. Mitchell Sharp, made a statement on May 22, in which, among other things, he said:

> "... we are very distressed and concerned that this latest member of the nuclear club should be a country with which successive Canadian Governments have carried over the past two decades extensive cooperation in the nuclear-energy field. This longstanding cooperation with India in the nuclear energy field has involved the gift, under the Colombo Plan, of a nuclear-research reactor; the provision of credit, expertise, materials and fuel for two electricity-generating reactors, and a variety of technical exchanges and training of personnel, etc. All of this assistance was intended to help India in meeting the critical energy needs of the Indian people and was provided to, and accepted by, India on the basis that it would be used for peaceful purposes only. We have made it clear in international discussions and in bilateral exchanges with India that the creation of a nuclear explosion for so-called peaceful purposes could not be considered as a peaceful purpose within the meaning of our cooperative arrangements.[28]

Foreign Minister Sharp then announced that Canada had suspended shipments of nuclear material and equipment to India, and had instructed Atomic Energy of Canada Ltd., the State corporation in charge of energy programs, to stop cooperating with India in the area of nuclear reactor projects and other technological exchange arrangements.

India was vehement in her protests. On May 25, Prime Minister Gandhi, addressing a public meeting in New Delhi, said: "Is it the contention that it is all right for the rich to use nuclear energy for destruction but not right for a poor country to find out whether it can be used for construction?"[29]

The Canadian government agreed in 1956, under the Columbo Plan, to have Atomic Energy of Canada Ltd. assist India in establishing a small 40-megawatt research reactor, named Cirus, in the Rajasthan region of India. At the same time Canada volunteered to train Indian technicians at Nuclear Laboratories in Ontario. Under the agreement signed in New Delhi on April 28 by Prime Minister Nehru and the Canadian High Commissioner Escott Reid, the cost of the project was to be shared by the two countries. Canada pledged to underwrite about $7.5 million of the estimated nearly $14 million total cost, while India was asked to pay $6.5 million. It was Canada who supplied the reactor's first load of fuel.[30]

The United States was also a contributor in this initial effort to help India toward possible energy production for peaceful uses. The U.S. Atomic Energy Commission sold India 42,000 pounds of heavy water in 1956 for the specific purpose of running the Cirus reactor.

India has four research reactors in operation today; Cirus is the largest. It is fueled by natural uranium instead of enriched uranium, and it is moderated by heavy water. These factors have worked in favor of India. She has deposits of natural uranium on her own soil, thus she does not have to import comparatively expensive enriched uranium. India has been producing its own heavy water in large quantities since 1965. Also, scientific opinion has it that natural uranium reactors produce more plutonium, the crucial substance for bomb production, than do conventional light water reactors of comparable power.[31]

Canada does not challenge the fact that it was Indian scientists alone who put together the nuclear device that was detonated in 1974. That India has the technical know-how is widely recognized. What Canadian officials suspect and resent is that the plutonium used in the explosion came from the research reactor Cirus. While this is possible, it was done under circumstances which were considered by India as neither subject to the Indo-Canadian Treaty of 1956 nor any other international control.

According to the original transaction between Canada and India it was expected that the reactor would be used for atomic research and experimental purposes—specifically for fundamental research in physical, chemical, biological and metallurgical problems relating to atomic energy. Beyond this the agreement placed no restrictions on India. It made no mention of international safeguards, because at the time the agreement came into force, no international safeguards had been established.[32]

During the first few years after India received the reactor, Canada supplied the fuel for its operation. Under this arrangement the agreement obligated India to give a full accounting of the resulting plutonium. The Indian officials maintain that this part of the agreement became inoperative in the 1960s when India started manufacturing her own fuel. India claimed that plutonium extracted under these conditions was hers and she could put it to whatever use she saw fit.

Canada took note of the talk of Indian scientists, in the late 1960s, of building a "peaceful bomb." General E. L. M. Burns, Canada's representative to the Geneva disarmament talks in the summer of 1966, stated at one of the meetings that from their point of view "peaceful uses" of nuclear energy prohibited any form of explosions. Indian representatives did not accept this version. It is reported that after General Yahya Khan, then president of Pakistan, complained to Prime Minister Pierre Trudeau that Pakistan was quite disturbed by the fact that Canada exercised little control over the use of her nuclear aid to India, the Canadian prime minister urged Mrs. Gandhi to sign the nuclear Nonproliferation Treaty. India's prime minister is said to have conveyed to her Canadian counterpart that Indian interpretation of the Indo-Canadian agreement did not rule out nuclear explosions for peaceful purposes, and that India would not sign the NPT as long as China and France refused to do so.[33]

Canada is a signatory to the 1968 nuclear Nonproliferation Treaty. As such she is somewhat guilt-ridden that she supplied the wherewithal which permitted India to make the nuclear breakthrough. Canada is also unhappy because she feels strongly that even if India has not violated the original Indo-Canadian agreement in law, she certainly has violated it in spirit. Leaders of India continue to deny this.

The United Nations General Assembly in its resolution of June 21, 1968, recommended to the nations of the world signature of the Treaty on Nonproliferation of nuclear weapons earlier negotiated and drafted by the United States and the Soviet Union. The treaty, signed on July 1, 1968, by the United States, the Soviet Union, Britain and 59 other nations, went into force in March, 1970. To date 106 nations have signed the treaty, out of which 83 have also ratified it. Twenty-three have signed it but have not yet ratified it, including Japan and Egypt. Prominent among those who have steadfastly refused to sign the treaty are China, France, India, Israel, Pakistan, South Africa, Argentina, and Brazil.

The substance of the Nonproliferation Treaty rests in the main in the following features.[34] First, the treaty commits the nuclear weapon states (U.S., USSR, Britain, France, China) to not transfer nuclear weapons or other nuclear explosive devices, or control over them, to any other party. It also enjoins the nuclear powers not to assist any other state in the manufacture of nuclear weapons. Second, the treaty secures a pledge from the nations that do not possess nuclear weapons that they will neither manufacture nor acquire them by any means or from any source including states not adhering to the treaty. Third, each nuclear weapon state party to the treaty is asked to make available "potential benefits from any peaceful applications of nuclear explosions" to any nonnuclear weapon states who have signed the treaty, subject to appropriate international control. Fourth, the treaty places a moral obligation on all signatory nations to undertake negotiations to put an end to the nuclear arms race and move forward toward complete disarmament under effective international control.

India has rejected the treaty on multiple grounds. She maintains that the treaty seeks to preserve the exclusive status of the nuclear weapon powers, thus according them undue influence over the rest of the world. India's policymakers also believe that the treaty discriminates heavily against nonnuclear weapon states. While they are forbidden to develop nuclear programs without international supervision, the nuclear weapon states remain free not only to multiply their weapons, but to continue research toward developing more sophisticated and devastating devices.

The treaty urges the states to initiate steps towards nuclear disarmament. From the Indian point of view the progress made by the United States and the Soviet Union in several summit meetings on this issue is sorely disappointing. Salt I talks, the Moscow summit in June, 1974, and the Vladivostok Ford-Brezhnev agreement in November, 1974, have resulted in ceilings on delivery systems and missiles. But no qualitative or quantitative inhibitions have been placed on the production of nuclear weapons. These meetings did not bring agreement on the part of the two superpowers to stop the arms race. The Moscow summit, aimed at curbing underground testing, produced an agreement that permitted unlimited underground testing until 1976. It tolerates detonation of nuclear devices underground up to the magnitude of 150 kilotons after 1976. As one author observed, this ". . . unfortunately suggests that the superpowers are not very serious about deemphasizing nuclear weapons."[35]

Also, the NPT calls for supervision by an international agency of facilities of nonnuclear weapon nations, yet no such provision applies to the nuclear weapon states. Thus only the nonnuclear weapon states are called upon to compromise their sovereignty. Nuclear weapon powers remain immune from international inspection.[36]

Lastly, an important objection raised by India concerns the absence of any guarantees that a nuclear power will neither attack nor threaten a nonnuclear weapon nation. The Security Council did adopt a resolution on June 19, 1968, with the intention of allaying such fears. The Security Council resolution, recognizing that a nuclear attack would obligate especially the nuclear weapon-holding permanent members of the Security Council to act, welcomes the assurances given by certain states that they would come to the aid of the victim nation immediately.[37] But the resolution goes no further. India considers such a loose arrangement totally ineffective.

To encourage nonnuclear weapon states to sign the NPT, and to allay their fears about possible attack, the United States declared on July 17, 1968 that she would initiate immediate action in the Security Council to meet such a threat or aggression according to the provisions of the U.N. Charter.[38] However this too is a promise any nation seriously afraid of nuclear threat would find inadequate. As Prime Minister Gandhi has said:

> We must realize in the final analysis, the effectiveness of any such nuclear shield in the field of security would depend not on the spirit in which the nonnuclear powers accept the shield, but on the national and vital interests of the giver.[39]

India's successful detonation of a nuclear device strongly implies that even if all her objections had been met, she would have probably preferred to leave her options open. India is not unconcerned with the dangers of proliferation and even possible theft in the future. But her leadership definitely wished to have a free hand to explore what India could accomplish, with her nuclear energy program, to further her economic and strategic security. Whether the country has achieved a measure of economic and strategic advantage by the nuclear test is subject to varied assessments. Two things are clear, however. First, it is difficult to accuse India of being singularly guilty of having opened the door to further proliferation. Second, India has not become a threat or a menace to the security of her neighbors by testing a nuclear device.

The United States began sharing its nuclear resources with the world in 1954, with the firm belief that it was sharing the benefits of peaceful atomic power. Since then, some 30 countries including Brazil, West Germany, Yugoslavia, and Taiwan have already received American nuclear aid. Ironically, in June, 1974, even before the noise over the Indian test had died down, then president Richard Nixon announced in Cairo that the United States would give a 600-megawatt reactor to Egypt to produce nuclear energy for industrial uses. And to silence the uproar, the president announced on his next stop in Tel Aviv that Israel too would receive a similar reactor. The State Department did say that the United States would impose strict safeguards to prevent these countries from diverting nuclear energy towards production of nuclear weapons. But even if the new safeguards are near foolproof, the earlier agreements, lacking tight safeguards, leave room for any of the parties to the 30 different agreements to produce a bomb if they so desire. As one commentator put it: ". . . even the most rigid safeguards will not guarantee that Middle Eastern nations may not develop their own atom bombs from other material. Israel, for example, possesses a 26-megawatt reactor supplied by the French without safeguards; since it started operation in 1963 it could have produced enough plutonium for about ten atom bombs."[40]

Israeli President Ephraim Katzir said on December 1, 1974, that Israel had the potential to make an atomic weapon, "and if we need it we will do it."[41]

As Senator Adlai E. Stevenson III points out, there are over 500 nuclear reactors in operation in 45 countries. By 1980, these reactors will be capable of producing 300,000 to 450,000 kilograms of plutonium. Only five to six kilograms is enough to put together a bomb of the size dropped on Nagasaki and Hiroshima. The senator says further: ". . . Salesmen from Canada, West Germany, the United Kingdom, France and the United States are busy making their rounds. The competition is intense. . . . Westinghouse and General Electric reactors know no national boundaries. Through a French venture, Westinghouse reactors find their way to Iran and wherever else the French can make a sale."[42]

It is widely accepted that the difference between a nuclear explosion carried out for peaceful purposes and one that might be carried out for the purposes of testing a nuclear weapon is practically none. Thus some states take it for granted that India now possesses the atom bomb. Contrary to this view India insists that she will not develop nuclear weapons. In an exclusive interview with *Newsweek's* foreign editor in late May, 1974, Prime Minister Gandhi said:

> There is a difference between a nuclear country and a nuclear-weapons country; we are not a nuclear-weapons country; we don't have any bombs. We don't intend to use this knowledge or this power for any other than peaceful purposes. Our neighbors need have no fear. We view the explosion as an extension of our work of research and keeping abreast of developments in science and technology; we have not viewed it in light of strengthening or creating fear or prestige or pride.[43]

Swaran Singh, at the time India's external affairs minister, told the U.N. General Assembly on September 26, 1974 "... We have no intention of making nuclear weapons."[44]

With due skepticism one can say that the true character of the nuclear device tested by India is in question. Nonetheless, the explosion alone cannot be equated with instant ability on the part of India to threaten or attack any of her neighbors. She will be restrained, as in the past, either willfully or by external influences.

This, of course, leads one to search for the reasons which spurred India to explode the device. The comments of George Quester warrant attention:

> India may indeed have built her bomb for peaceful uses, although all the outside world doubts this. She may have acted in part to intimidate Pakistan or to prepare the psychological climate for future negotiations with China. The bomb may also have been built to win prestige and some general political clout, to bolster Mrs. Gandhi's domestic political position, to win India greater respect abroad.[45]

India could have detonated the device for any one or all of the reasons cited above. It is also possible that the real reasons lie in the events of 1971, on the eve of the Indo-Pak war. As the situation in the then two wings of Pakistan, East and West, assumed ugly proportions and India saw herself being drawn into a war on the side of East Pakistan, now Bangladesh, the New Delhi government sought ways to prevent China from intervening on West Pakistan's side. Inasmuch as the Indian government was informed by the American officials that India could not expect help from the United States if China entered the fray between India and Pakistan, India looked for other avenues to thwart China. In August, 1971, India signed a defense treaty with the Soviet Union to accomplish her objective. It was at this time that India's policymakers also decided to proceed with full-speed production of a nuclear device. As the five powers did before her, India based that decision on her perception that future security needs left no other choice.

Preparations for India's first nuclear test were two years in the making. The blast occurred in 1974 because the scientists were ready, and also because the regime of Prime Minister Gandhi considered the moment opportune.

Even if India has not yet produced the bomb itself, it is quite clear that she can readily acquire a sizeable number, because in addition to the technology she presently has a formidable complex of independent sources of nuclear energy.

The Atomic Energy Establishment at Trombay, on the west coast, has developed the use of atomic energy for producing electricity which is presently being utilized for industry and irrigation.

The Rajasthan Atomic Power Plant, the facility at Tarapur in Maharashtra, and another power station at Kalpakkam near Madras are currently generating approximately 2,000 megawatts of nuclear power.

The two 200-megawatt power reactors nearing completion at Kalpakkam have the same design as the Canadian reactors. But these are being built by Indian scientists without any outside help. The plutonium produced by these reactors will not be subject to international control.

The Defense Minister told the Indian Parliament in May, 1972, that the Atomic Energy Commission aims to increase nuclear power production to 2,700 megawatts before 1980.[46]

According to an Indian government report published in 1973, there are 10,400 persons employed at the Bhabha Atomic Research Center at Trombay and other plutonium processing and electronics manufacturing facilities. Of these, 2,400 are highly qualified scientists. Given these assets India should have the capacity to produce about 175 kilograms of plutonium a year. This is enough for some 36 explosives of the size dropped on Nagasaki and Hiroshima.[47]

Two factors, however, make relevance of this nuclear capability doubtful as an effective instrument of foreign policy implementation. First, if and when India builds nuclear weapons, whether she will have the will to use them remains uncertain. Second, without a sophisticated delivery system, her nuclear arsenal will have serious limitations.

Inasmuch as India vehmently rejects the idea of a "nuclear freezone" in South Asia, as well as any other constraints that might impose external supervision on her nuclear energy program, this may indicate that she does not wish to rule out the production of a nuclear weapon in the future. For the present then, possibly all India has sought to achieve is to make it clear that she can and will produce nuclear weapons to fight any pressures that China and Pakistan might thrust upon her, individually or cooperatively.

India's Economic Capability

India's poverty is legend, although the root causes of her economic ills are little known and even less understood by anyone except the experts. Various estimates and surveys appear to indicate that India does not lack the basic resources. But she seems to have failed at arresting her population growth and utilizing her resources to the fullest extent.

At the base India remains an agrarian society. Approximately

80 percent of her present 600 million population live in some 567,000 villages. Thus nearly five out of every six Indians live in a rural environment, and farming is the major occupation of most of them.[48] Agriculture is the chief industry of India, supplying nearly half the national income and jobs for some 70 percent of the working population.

The average landholding of the Indian farmer is seven acres. But nearly five million farmers each hold less than a half-acre. The average farmer continues to plow the fields with a wooden stick, at times fitted with a half-inch steel tip, pulled by a pair of bullocks. Modern tractors or other farm machinery are rare, and Indian farmers as a whole have exhibited little enthusiasm so far either for the modern methods of farming or the implements. The result is that the agricultural yields in India are among the lowest in the world and the largest portion of what the farmer produces is consumed by his family.[49] India's economists maintain that the food the villagers eat makes up 66 percent of their total income.

As much as three-quarters of the cultivated land is used for food crops, with one-quarter being devoted to such cash crops as cotton, jute, oil seeds, and tobacco. But despite the large acreage given to rice and wheat, India has thus far failed to feed her millions on her own. In 1970–71 the food crop was 108.4 million tons. This was the year of the "Green Revolution," and national leaders proclaimed that India had finally achieved self-sufficiency in food production. But since then the annual crop production has been a disappointing three to ten million tons below the 1970–71 level. In 1971–72 the annual production was 105.2 million tons. In 1972–73 the figure was even lower and stood at 95.2 million tons. While the food production for the year 1973–74 did rise to 105 million tons, the population between the years 1970 through 1974 had increased by 35 million. With all these additional mouths to feed, the food production had gone down by three million tons.[50]

The Indian Ministry of Agriculture, in its annual report for the year 1973–74, blamed the food shortages on widespread draught and short supplies of fertilizer and oil.[51] This being the case, the prospect for self-sufficiency in food production looks bleak for many years to come.

In 1966 India produced nearly 1.5 million tons of fertilizer. The aim of the fourth Five Year Plan was to double this quantity by 1973, but the output was two million tons by the target date. This was not only one million tons short of the goal, it was half the quantity India requires to meet her needs. Indian fertilizer plants are operating at only 60 percent capacity at present, primarily due to power and oil shortages, and it is unlikely that the situation will improve in the near future.[52]

The oil crisis made a mark on a worldwide basis in 1974. But the developing countries were the hardest hit, India among them. Ninety percent of the total petroleum used by India is expended on essential industrial, transport, and agricultural services. Estimates are that India will be importing two-thirds of its oil requirements for quite some time, despite some optimistic predictions made on the basis of recent explorations carried out by an American drilling team. Indian diplomatic effort did bear some fruit: She signed oil agreements with Iran and Iraq in 1974, which will permit her to purchase up to 30 percent of her import needs from these two countries on a deferred-payment plan.[53] But this does not solve the long-range problem.

Of all the people gainfully employed in India, fewer than ten percent earn their livelihood from industry. Merely 19.9 percent of the population live in cities and towns of more than 5,000. Some one hundred cities have a population of more than 100,000 each, while only eight cities have a population of more than a million each.

Beginnings of industrialization in India go as far back as 1850, with the development of coal mines, cotton-textile mills and jute mills. Tata Iron and Steel Works, best known of the privately owned industrial enterprises of India, was established in 1906. But the number of factory workers amounted to only 900,000 in 1914. It was between the two world wars, after the British saw fit to introduce protective tariffs in 1921 for the first time, when a variety of light industries sprang up in India. Cement, rubber, leather, glass, paper, and soap production began during this period. And while chemicals, sewing machines, bicycles, electric motors, transformers, diesel engines, and some machine tools were being manufactured before World War II ended, there was virtually no capital machinery being produced in India prior to independence. As Chandrasekhar has written: "Until almost the end of the British rule the Indian economy was a typical colonial one. She tended to produce and export, in the main, raw materials, and foodstuffs and to import textiles, iron and steel goods, machinery, and miscellaneous manufactures of a wide variety."[54] The policymakers of independent India were therefore saddled with the task of establishing an industrial base essential for a modern economy while achieving agricultural goals to meet the demands of an ever-growing population.

Starting in 1951, a series of five-year economic plans introduced by the government has encouraged development of a host of new industries producing such commodities as automobiles, railway coaches, radios, telephone equipment, and even certain types of aircraft.

Stressing heavy industrialization in the second Five-Year Plan (1956–61), the Indian government made increased steel production one of its major goals. On the one hand the private steel concern of Tata Iron and Steel Works was urged to double its production, while on the other hand the government with assistance of foreign capital started to build publicly-owned steel plants. In addition to the Tata Steel Works, India today has three plants built in the public sector with the help of governments of West Germany, Great Britain, and the Soviet Union. With the aid of the Soviet Union, construction is already under way for a fourth publicly owned steel plant. The Rourkhela plant, the Durgapur plant, and the Bhilai plant have helped boost the steel production of India to 10 million tons a year, making India Asia's third largest steel producer after Japan and China.[55]

Independent India's planners have also emphasized irrigation and production of hydroelectric power, resulting in the completion of the Bhakra Nangal project, which includes one of the highest dams in the world and will produce at peak capacity electric power of 1050 megawatts; the Damodar Valley project, which includes several hydroelectric power houses, as well as three thermal power stations, located at the heart of India's chief industrial area; and the Hirakud and Tungabhardra projects.

As discussed earlier, India has also launched atomic energy programs which place her among those few nation states which are already tapping atomic energy for peaceful purposes. But as of today, fifty percent of India's energy needs are met through noncommercial sources such as cow-dung and firewood, twenty-five percent are met by coal and electricity, while the remaining twenty-five percent are supplied by petroleum products.[56]

Thus during the last two and a half decades, while India is considered tenth among the industrial states of the world, she has been unsuccessful at providing adequate goods and services for all her citizens. She has failed to put them to creative use on the farm, in the factory, and in the army, in a manner which would make her rapidly increasing population an asset rather than a liability.[57]

India's Gross National Product stood at $78.6 billion in 1973. Japan's GNP during the same year was $439.1 billion; and Japan has to serve a population which is only one-fifth of India's.[58] India's per capita gross national product stands at $90 today, whereas Japan's per capita GNP stands at $760 and Israel's at $1,130. Out of some 135 countries in the world, India is 95th in total production and per capita income. In 1968–69 the per capita income of an Indian was $81 as compared with average per capita income of $2,290 for the developed countries and $180 for the developing countries. Her increase in aggregate national income was 2.2 percent in 1968–69, 5.3 percent in 1969–70, and 4.7 percent in 1970–71. Even today only

15 percent of India's more than half a million villages have access to electricity.[59]

India's unemployment rate is staggering. In 1971 the total number of unemployed workers was 21.5 million. Out of this 19.3 million were rural unemployed. This represents nine percent of the total labor force. If one were to add to this the numbers which are in the category of "underemployed," it is estimated by Ford Foundation experts that "man years" of unemployment per year would rise to 60 to 70 million.[60]

India's economic woes are compounded by the fact that over the years, to the present, she has been spending the largest portion of her foreign exchange on the purchase of food abroad. During 1974 she was compelled to import some four million tons of food grains. The rise in oil costs and the continued need for importation of fertilizers has made the problem even more difficult to solve. The then finance minister, Y. B. Chavan, told the annual World Bank meeting on September 30, 1974, that India faced a situation in which nearly 80 percent of her export earning will be wiped out that year on imports of three commodities—oil, fertilizer and food.[61] And inasmuch as India continues to import all her heavy machinery needs, whether for civilian or military use, from countries of Eastern Europe and Western Europe, her foreign exchange situation is worsening. A recent study commissioned by the International Bank for Reconstruction and Development indicates that India, Pakistan, Brazil, Mexico, Indonesia, and some other countries, all owe more than $2,000 million each. Further, India, Pakistan, and Mexico, among others, need to spend at least 20 percent of their annual export earnings to service past debts. In most cases debts are rising faster than either total output or export earnings. India is finding it more and more difficult every year to repay the debt, which at present stands close to seven billion dollars.

India does not lack basic raw materials. Geological surveys indicate that she has some of the world's largest deposits of high-grade iron ore and coal, and oil reserves have been discovered recently in Assam and Gujrat. India has signed an agreement with Rumania for assistance in developing an oil industry. American firms are supplying the equipment to tap this oil. If successful, this source could provide one million tons of crude. In addition to her 1974 arrangements with Iran and Iraq, India is trying hard to boost exports to Gulf States such as Kuwait, Muscat, and Abu Dhabi with the hope of relieving the pressure of mounting oil costs. India's reserves of bauxite, an essential alloy for aluminum, are the second largest in the world. Until 1954, India was the main supplier of manganese for the United States. Along with Brazil and Malagasy Republic, India continues to be the major supplier of this metal, necessary for making steel, to all of Western Europe. She also appears to have ample quantities of rare minerals like chromite, thorium, ilemenite, gypsum and mica. But it is mainly the absence of industrial management and technology, skilled labor, and capital, that have prevented India from making rapid progress toward industrialization. It is also apparent that political leadership has failed to provide the incentives which enable a government to mobilize the country's human and material resources to the fullest extent.

Apparently India has not succeeded so far in striking that crucial balance between production of consumer goods, capital goods, and defense equipment that characterizes the economic capability of a respectable power among nation states.

Influence of Military and Economic Capability on India's Foreign Policy

India's military and economic capability has influenced her foreign policy in a variety of ways. During her several military confrontations, she learned what tremendous problems arise when a nation state lacks the requisite military and economic resources. The 1971 conflict was a unique experience for India. She felt satisfied that she had succeeded in building a relatively effective military machine, but she had yet to reach self-sufficiency in the area of her military or economic needs. Even with the improved military capability it was questionable whether she had an effective deterrent force against China, or Pakistan in collaboration with China. It is also true that part of her improved power position rested on her alliance with the Soviet Union, an alliance with, at best, positive and negative sides to it. While India has detonated a nuclear device, the value and effectiveness of her atomic power as an instrument of foreign policy is very much in the air.

In 1961 India successfully won Goa from the colonial control of Portugal when Portugal failed to meet India's military challenge with equal force. However, in 1962 she suffered a humiliating defeat when she attempted to prevent China from continuing to occupy territory claimed by India under treaty right. She has since lived under the constant threat of a renewed Chinese attack.[62]

India's next experience came in 1965. A confrontation between Indian and Pakistani troops in Kashmir led to a widening of the conflict with the result that India opened a second front along the entire boundary of West Pakistan adjoining India. As India verged on military success, which could have possibly helped her secure a solution to the Kashmir problem, Britain and the United States imposed a strict economic and military embargo against both antagonists which compelled them to halt fighting. India's leaders were enraged but helpless. They realized that reliance upon outside powers for crucial military and economic supplies placed serious limitations on India's foreign policy.

Given India's development problems, and further given the 2.5 percent yearly increase in population with no concomitant growth in agricultural output, emphasis on civilian production over defense production clearly remained a part of all planning. Thus India's dependence on foreign capital, as well as defense equipment from abroad, swayed her foreign policy.

To a large degree independent India's posture of nonalignment as a response to the cold war pressures from the U.S.A. and USSR can be attributed to her belief that a posture of friendship toward both camps would draw economic aid from both sides.

India's attempts to use moral force as a major instrument of foreign policy can also be ascribed to her lack of military and economic power. As Prime Minister Nehru stated before the Indian Parliament: "The strength which limits or, at any rate, conditions the foreign policy of a country may be military, financial or, if I may use the word, moral. It is obvious that India has neither military nor financial strength."[63] The behavioral pattern of nation states on the international scene, however, also reflects the fact that use of moral force without the manifest presence of military and economic force in the background has little effectiveness in the long run. For while India's use of moral force did gain influence for her in the international arena for several years, with the passage of time her military and economic weakness began to have a telling effect on her relations with other nations.

India's influence with Asian and African states diminished considerably in the aftermath of the 1962 Chinese attack. What is even more significant is the fact that Asian and African states as a whole neither condemned the Chinese action nor did any of these states offer even token assistance to India.

In December, 1971, India found the opportunity to reverse growing world opinion of her as a weak and ineffective nation state. India's success in splitting Pakistan, and the emergence of Bangladesh, was evidence that India's military machine had grown in size and effectiveness. The performance was impressive; India had scored a decisive military victory. More than that, she had maneuvered her relations with the major powers so that the U.S. and China could not come to the aid of Pakistan because of the possible implications of Indo-Soviet Treaty of 1971.[64] In order to avoid a direct confrontation with the Soviet Union, the United States allowed Pakistan, her old and faithful military ally and a member of SEATO, to lose more than half of her territory. To avoid risking a border clash with the Soviet Union, China thumped her chest in support of her new found friend Pakistan, but moved not a finger to help her. India could thus claim with reason that her military strength was of no inferior caliber. She could also claim that now she knew how to deploy it far better than was the case in the past.

Despite India's victory, however, there were observers who were quick to point to the fact that India's newborn confidence and nerve could not be accepted without qualification. It was partly India's good fortune that prevented her from suffering a military disaster as a result of the preemptive strike by Pakistan on December 3, 1971. India's early warning system proved ineffective. Pakistani fighter-bombers penetrated Indian territory and attacked airfields as far inland as the city of Agra, a few hundred miles east of New Delhi, the nation's capital. The enemy planes were not challenged because even though they were detected on the Indian radar screens along the frontiers, the rest of the country could not be alerted. This is because the telephone network is the only medium available at present to relay such information—and the long-distance telephone wires have failed to operate properly on repeated occasions. Indian Air Force planners, conscious of this weakness, had provided the proper shielding for the planes on the ground.

In October, 1973, India signed an agreement with the United States to correct this communication problem. On the basis of an $18 million loan provided by the U.S. Defense Department, India has contracted an American firm to build a vast microwave communication system that will bolster the country's air defense against a surprise attack by Pakistan or China. While this project, with the code name Peace Indigo, will eventually link together radar stations all across the Indian territory, it may not be completed until 1977.[65]

The war with Pakistan was by no means a total war. Pakistan had retained most of her armed strength in West Pakistan, and Indian and Pakistani forces did not engage in full scale battle in the west. Pakistani armies in East Pakistan, separated from their western brethren by 1,000 miles of territory which is all Indian, remained almost completely cut off from any effective assistance from the west. The most important factor in the situation was that the Bengali population of East Pakistan, calling their land Bangladesh, was in nationwide revolt against West Pakistan. The Freedom Fighters of Bangladesh gave major support in the quick victory achieved by the Indian armies. And without Russian backing which kept China and America out of the fray, India might have found it difficult to accomplish what she did. Such reminders only partially reduce the credit that is due to the policymakers of India and the Indian armies.

Nonetheless, these aspects highlight the fact that India still lacks the offensive capability to deal with major situations.

Undeniably, India's success at exploding a nuclear device has added a new dimension to her capability factor. If the policymakers stick by their currently stated aims of confining their nuclear ability to peaceful tasks, India's military equation will not alter radically. On the other hand, if they perceive that their hand is being forced to produce nuclear weapons, it could lead to a significant change in India's prowess and foreign policy. But even then it is questionable as to how far India can go to equip herself with a nuclear arsenal.

Of course, a nuclear arsenal would have very limited value without a sophisticated delivery system and missiles to carry the nuclear warheads. India is actively involved in researching some of these areas. In June, 1974, India launched an experimental space rocket manufactured at the Vikram Sarahhai Space Center at Trivandrum in South India. The rocket carried a payload of 70 Kgs and reached an altitude of about 120 Km.[66] The Indian Space Research Organization launched India's first artificial satellite in 1975 with the agreed-upon assistance of the Soviet Academy of Sciences. The satellite, weighing over 300 Kgs, was launched from somewhere in Russian territory by a Soviet rocket. Not only are these just the beginnings of a program which requires extensive development to reach a meaningful stage, but even here India's reliance on outside sources shows once again how distant she is from being a nuclear-weapon state in the real sense.

As one Indian scientist has observed: "I am of the view that India can produce a nuclear bomb as a result of a crash program.... As for the delivery systems, the picture is more dismal. One way is to deliver the bomb by a conventional bomber, but I doubt if the bombers in our fleet are capable of doing so. As to the indigenous development of missiles, the picture is even more dismal. Our amateur missile designers, under the guidance of generalist scientists and semieducated military generals, have not been able to successfully develop an antitank missile. We have been informed that we are producing one under license. Such a missile uses only visual and simple optical guidance. The air-to-air missiles are again being produced under license and the ground-to-air missiles have been acquired abroad.

"Production under license does not mean that we are dependent only for design, but also for essential raw materials, components, systems and subsystems. Thus indigenous production is virtually an assembly system."[67]

There is, of course, the ever-present question of whether India can afford the cost of a full-blown nuclear arsenal. Many an eyebrow was raised when India exploded the nuclear device: There was a strong feeling in several quarters that a country as poor as India should not have diverted badly needed resources for greater agricultural and industrial production towards such an exercise. While different sources mentioned totally different cost estimates, Dr. H. N. Sethna, chairman of the Atomic Energy Commission of India, put the cost close to half a million dollars and suggested that in view of the immense energy needs India might realize when the knowledge from the test is put to practical use, the expenditure was well worth it.[68] Prime Minister Gandhi said: ". . . no new budgetary provision was made for it. There was no foreign exchange expenditure. And there was no dependence on any other country."[69] Even if one accepts the conservative estimate given by Indian officials, it is quite clear that producing missiles and a delivery system will involve tens of billions of dollars which would depress India's economic and social progress to the point of causing serious economic dislocation and social discontent. The resulting political instability could prove disastrous.

India is clearly decades behind the Western powers in electronic, aerospace, submarine, radar, and missile technologies. Thus even if she possesses the bomb or comes to possess it soon, she has no clout usually associated with a nuclear-weapon state. Her nuclear capability neither upsets the world balance of power nor does it give her influence in global politics.

The testing of the device did, however, earn for India a measure of prestige at home and abroad—more so at home than abroad. Coming on the heels of her victory in the Indo-Pak war, the test made India feel confident of a dominant position on the subcontinent of South Asia. While one may hope that the atomic explosion would advance India's independence from Soviet influence, chances are that Indian reliance on the USSR will continue, primarily because China remains hostile to India, and India certainly has no deterrence to match the Chinese nuclear capability. China already possesses a hydrogen bomb and IRBMs, and is expected to have ICBMs in the near future. Admittedly, the ability to explode a nuclear device could enable India to quickly close those Himalayan passes through which the Chinese advanced in 1962, were they to launch on a similar course again. A modest nuclear arsenal could further provide India with the capacity to create necessary conditions to force the involvement of great powers. But again, in the final analysis India would still have to turn to powers with nuclear capability superior to that of China; and in the presence of the Indo-Soviet treaty of 1971, Russia appears to be the likely choice.

On May 28, 1974, soon after her nuclear experiment, India signed an agreement with Argentina for cultural exchanges and cooperation in the peaceful use of atomic energy.[70] An Argentine spokesman is reported to have said that the agreement could contribute to the construction of a third nuclear power plant for Argentina. This indicates that as one of the most advanced countries in nuclear technology among the Third World nations, India could extend her diplomatic leverage by exporting nuclear technology to those developing states which wish to make rapid progress in their own nuclear energy programs. India could also use this channel to barter for badly needed economic resources. But these appear to be the outer limits of what India can accomplish presently with her newly acquired nuclear ability.

Therefore, while India has the fourth largest army in the world today, she cannot take the military initiative to secure her interests against neighboring China or Pakistan, the two countries against whom she still holds territorial claims. The two billion dollar defense budget introduced by the government in the Parliament in 1972–73 is six times the 374 million dollars defense outlay accepted by the government of India in 1960–61, the year prior to the boundary war with China. India's defense budget stood at two percent of the national income in 1947. It has now climbed to the level of nearly seven percent of national income and is more than twenty percent of the total federal budget. But considering the rather low level of Indian national income, which stands at $90 per capita, the everpresent tension on the domestic scene born of religious, regional, and economic rivalries, and the fact that India has to guard a land and sea frontier line of 11,700 miles, India's defense spending when compared to other countries, is even now less than formidable. If India comes to possess nuclear weapons, that will certainly change the character of her military power. But how it will improve her ability to influence regional and world politics will depend entirely on the nature and size of her nuclear arsenal. On the basis of her present priorities, one could speculate that during the next decade or so India will not go beyond the acquisition of a minimum nuclear capability that will further bolster her defense vis à vis China and Pakistan, but would be far short of any offensive capability.

India's economic development has been slow and inadequate. With greater population pressure the situation could become explosive. If the U.S., the USSR, Australia, and Canada had not come to India's aid in 1974 with supplies of badly needed food grains, many parts of India would have suffered large-scale starvation. She is still dependent upon outside powers for more modern and sophisticated weapons, a serious handicap. Realistically breaking with her past policies, India has come to rely very heavily upon the Soviet Union, both militarily and economically. Soviet party chief Leonid Brezhnev's visit to India in November, 1973, ended with a 15 year Indo-Soviet economic agreement for further development of economic and trade cooperation between the two countries. While details of the various agreements were not released, one of them relates to cooperation and consultation between the planning agencies of the Soviet Union and India. A top Soviet official commented: "The Planning principle adopted in the agreement is the Soviet one, and the Indians have accepted it. In essence this means there will be extremely close Indo-Soviet planning cooperation for at least the next 15 years."[71]

This development will easily have the dual effect of making India feel secure against a possible attack from her unfriendly neighbors, but at the same time restraining her freedom of diplomatic maneuver—notwithstanding all public statements of Indian leaders to the contrary.

India has expressed great concern over the recent activities of Russian and American navies in the Indian Ocean. While the Russian naval strength in the area was relatively low until 1970, the Soviet Union has been rapidly increasing her presence in the Indian Ocean, partly to contain China and partly to fill the vacuum left by British naval departure. Persuaded by somewhat the same rationale, America has begun countermoves. The U.S. has started to build a naval base on the island of Diego Garcia, a part of the Chagos archipelago, located some 1,200 miles south of the tip of India in the Indian Ocean. The American government showed interest in this area in the 1960s, when the British made it known that they intended to phase out their military presence in the Indian Ocean. But reports of increasing Soviet presence have spurred the demand for a matching presence on the part of America. During the "global alert" called by President Nixon in October 1973, a U.S. aircraft task group was sent to the Indian Ocean to challenge a potential Soviet military intervention in the Middle East. When the alert was over, it was revealed by the defense secretary that the U.S. Navy would not be called back, and that it would continue to patrol the area from then on. Some congressional representatives are of the opinion that Diego Garcia is bound to become one of America's major naval bases abroad. This is exactly what the littoral states in the area fear. India has been vocal in demanding that both the Soviet Union and the United States keep out of the Indian Ocean. The superpowers have ignored all protests.

India has no ability to guard her oceanfront on her own against a powerful adversary. It is rumored that the USSR would expect naval facilities in return for economic and military aid. Will she eventually yield to Russian pressure in this area as she discovers that she has once again no other choice?

Fast moving developments in today's world do not permit easy predictions. One can, however, make a few observations given the basic ingredients of India's political and economic environment. India's military capability has improved greatly over the years. But her experiences in military conflict in the last twenty-five years or more confirm the fact that her role in world politics must remain limited. Even as a regional power she will remain constrained by the presence of powerful China on her northern borders, the ever-present threat of a possible alliance between China and Pakistan, and the growing control over the Indian Ocean by Russia and America. Present Indian capability gives the country some room to maneuver her policies nearer at home, in South Asia and Southeast Asia. But it does not permit India to play that role on the world scene to which she became accustomed during the early Nehru years.

Notes

[1] *Peace and War* (New York: Doubleday & Co., 1966), p. 40.
[2] For a detailed discussion, see the core volume in this series by David Wilkinson.
[3] Lorne J. Kavic, *India's Quest for Security: Defense Policies 1947–1965* (Berkeley: University of California Press, 1967), p. 25.
[4] Michael Brecher, *India and World Politics* (New York: Frederick A. Praeger, 1968), p. 167.
[5] Jawaharlal Nehru, *Independence and After* (New York: The John Day Company, 1950), p. 213.
[6] Jawaharlal Nehru, *India's Foreign Policy* (New Delhi: The Publications Division, Government of India, 1961), p. 13.
[7] *The Untold Story* (New Delhi: Allied Publishers, 1967), p. 348.
[8] *Seminar*, New Delhi, 1962.
[9] *Jawaharlal Nehru's Speeches* (New Delhi: The Publications Division, Government of India, 1954), p. 230.
[10] Reported by K. P. S. Menon, onetime Indian Ambassador to Russia.
[11] J. Bandyopadhyaya, *The Making of India's Foreign Policy* (New Delhi: Allied Publishers, 1970), p. 242.
[12] *The Sunday Standard* (New Delhi), January 30, 1972.
[13] H. M. Patel, *The Defense of India* (New York: Asia Publishing House, 1963), p. 13.
[14] President Rajendra Prasad in his address to the Parliament in January, 1950, said that the government wished to reduce defense expenditure for reasons of economy but could not do so because ". . . evil forces were endangering its [India's] security both within and from outside."
[15] *Indian Information*, April 1, 1949, p. 370.
[16] *Ibid.*, p. 341.
[17] Views expressed by General K. S. Thimayya, India's onetime Army Chief of Staff, on this subject merit attention. *Seminar*, New Delhi, July, 1962.
[18] Lorne J. Kavic, *India's Quest for Security: Defense Policies, 1947–1965* (Berkeley: University of California Press, 1967), p. 90.

[19] *After Nehru Who?* (New York: Harcourt, Brace and World, Inc., 1963), p. 267.
[20] *The Hindu,* (Madras), January 17, 1950.
[21] India was exporting arms and other defense equipment to Third World countries in the 1970s. In 1971 she sold arms worth $4.2 million to other nations. *Times of India* (New Delhi), May 12, 1972.
[22] These figures were selected from two main sources: data supplied by the Director of the Institute of Defense Studies and Analyses, New Delhi, to *The Times of India* during November, 1971, and data published by the London Institute of Strategic Studies in its annual volume *Military Balance.* There was minor variance in the two reports.
[23] *The Times of India* (New Delhi) May 3, 1972.
[24] *The Statesman* (Calcutta), May 20, 1974.
[25] *Los Angeles Times,* June 9, 1974, Part VI, p. 5.
[26] *The Times of India,* (New Delhi), May 23, 1974.
[27] *The Times of India,* (New Delhi), May 23, 1974.
[28] *Statement by the Secretary of State for external affairs, the Honourable Mitchell Sharp,* May 22, 1974, Department of External Affairs, Canada, p. 2.
[29] *India News,* Washington D.C., June 7, 1974.
[30] *Agreement on the Canada-India Columbo Plan Atomic Reactor Project.* Department of External Affairs, Canada.
[31] Robert Gillette, "India: Into the Nuclear Club on Canada's Shoulders," *Science,* Vol. 184, no. 4141, p. 1054.
[32] In the mid-sixties Canada sold two other reactors to India. These reactors were the Canadian CANDU type. In this transaction Canada volunteered to give India a loan of $82 million at a favorable 6 percent interest rate so that India could make the purchase. Also around the same period, the U.S. Atomic Energy Commission approved the sale of twin 190-megawatt boiling water reactors to India. These were supplied by General Electric. The American built reactors are fueled with enriched uranium while the Canadian ones are fueled by natural uranium. Both Canadian and U.S. officials feel certain that the plutonium used for the explosion by India was not diverted from these reactors, because agreements signed for the sale of these reactors contained safeguards. These reactors are under the supervision of the International Atomic Energy Agency, an arm of the United Nations.
[33] *The Hindu* (Madras), June 26, 1974.
[34] For a fuller understanding of this treaty, two books would be very helpful for the student: Mason Willrich, *Nonproliferation Treaty; Framework for Nuclear Arms Control* (Charlottesville, Va: Michie Co., 1969), and, Bennett Boskey and Mason Willrich (eds.), *Nuclear Proliferation: Prospects for Control* (Massachusetts: Cambridge University Press, 1970).
[35] George H. Quester, "Can Proliferation Now Be Stopped?" *Foreign Affairs,* Vol. 53, No. 1 October 1974, p. 86.
[36] The United States and the United Kingdom did offer to submit themselves to supervision and inspection of the same order as imposed upon the nonnuclear weapon states.

While no specific agreements have been executed to date, both the powers are in the process of working out an arrangement whereby they can place some nuclear facilities under the inspection of IAEA on restricted basis. West Germany, now a signatory to the NPT, is also seriously considering submitting itself to some supervision by IAEA. But the Soviet Union has never entertained the idea.

China and France, of course, remain outside the framework of the treaty. For a discussion of some of the problems associated with this issue see: Lawrence Scheinman, "EURATOM and the IAEA," *Nuclear Proliferation: Prospects for Control* (Massachusetts: Cambridge University Press, 1970). See also Lawrence Sheinman, "Political Implications of Safeguards," in Mason Willrich (editor), *International Safeguards and Nuclear Industry* (Baltimore: Johns Hopkins Press, 1973).

[37]*Nuclear Proliferation: Prospects for Control*, p. 159.

[38]*Ibid.*, p. 163.

[39]Quoted in Sheton L. Williams, *The U.S., India, and the Bomb* (Baltimore: The Johns Hopkins Press, 1969), p. 52. NATO provides the only example where an effective nuclear shield is supplied by a weapon-holding power for the protection of some nonnuclear weapon states. The nuclear weapons located in Europe are expected to serve NATO forces in the defense of Europe. Does this constitute a violation of that part of the Nonproliferation Treaty which prohibits the transfer of nuclear weapons to other countries? The question has never been raised in the U.N. NATO's interpretation and American reservations in this regard are noteworthy. See George Bunn, "Horizontal Proliferation of Nuclear Weapons," *Nuclear Proliferation: Prospects for Control*.

[40]*Newsweek*, July 1, 1974, p. 36.

[41]*Los Angeles Times*, December 3, 1974.

[42]Adlai E. Stevenson III, "Nuclear Reactors: America Must Act." *Foreign Affairs*, Vol. 53, No. 1, October, 1974, p. 65.

[43]*Newsweek*, June 3, 1974, p. 37.

[44]*India News*, Washington D.C., October 4, 1974.

[45]*Foreign Affairs, op. cit.*, pp. 80–81.

[46]*The Times of India* (New Delhi), May 3, 1972.

[47]As reported in *Science, op. cit.*

[48]The number of landless is estimated to be 45 million. They earn their livelihood as laborers. These laborers earn a wage as low as 7 to 10 cents a day.

[49]"Japan raises twice as many food crops per acre as China, and China's yield is nearly double that of India." Stated by S. Chandrasekhar in *American Aid and India's Economic Development* (New York: Frederick A. Praeger, 1965), p. 81.

[50]The information has been mainly drawn from *Illustrated Weekly of India*, Bombay, July 28 and August 11, 1974; and *Foreign Economic Trends: Their Implications for the U.S.* (Washington, D.C.: U.S. Dept. of Commerce, May 1974).

[51]*Illustrated Weekly of India*, Bombay, July 28, 1974.

[52]The information supplied here is from the U.S. Dept. of Commerce publication cited earlier.

[53]*Ibid.*

[54]S. Chandrasekhar, *op. cit.*, p. 15.

[55]Both India and China started in the 1940s with a steel production of a million tons a year. Today Chinese production has reached 21 million tons a year as opposed to India's 10 million tons. On his trip to India in December 1973, Soviet Party Chief Brezhnev expressed the hope that with Soviet help, India's new steel plant at Bokaro, billed as the largest metallurgical giant in South East Asia, will be soon producing 10 million tons of additional steel per year.

[56]*The Illustrated Weekly of India*, Bombay, August 11, 1974.

[57] If the present trend continues, Indians will number 900 million by 2000 A.D. India currently supports 41.8 percent of the world's population with only 2.4 percent of the world land area and 1.5 percent of world's income. India's population growth rate of 2.5 percent per annum is one of the highest in the world. "Today, 80 million Indian children out of a total of 150 million are mentally retarded because of malnutrition. Fourteen thousand of them go blind every year." *Democratic World*, New Delhi, May 3, 1973, p. 4.

[58] There are no official Chinese figures for GNP. Western estimates have varied greatly. According to the U.S. estimate, China's GNP stood at $140 billion in 1973. For detailed information see *Military Balance* (London: Institute of Strategic Studies, 1974).

[59] Most of the statistics were drawn from *Statistical Outline of India 1972-73* (Bombay: Tata Services Limited, October 1972).

[60] *Democratic World*, New Delhi, May 3, 1973, p. 2.

[61] *India News*, Washington, D.C., October 11, 1974.

[62] Reference here is to the boundary dispute between India and China, the source of the 1962 conflict. India claims that China has occupied territory south of the McMahon Line which established the boundaries between India, China and Tibet in 1914. China questions this. The British Government of India held a tripartite conference of Tibet, China and Britain in 1913 at Simla (India). The Simla Convention, which ended in April 1914, resulted in several agreements, one of which fixed the McMahon Line as the boundary between India and China. While the representatives of the three governments attending the Conference initialled the agreements, subsequently the Chinese government refused to sign the treaties. The validity of the boundary line as well as the treaties has, therefore, become a major issue between India and China.

[63] *Jawaharlal Nehru's Speeches 1949-1953* (New Delhi: The Publications Division, Ministry of Information & Broadcasting, 1954), p. 230.

[64] The Indo-Soviet Treaty, as well as the Indo-Pak war of 1971, are dealt with in greater detail in the last chapter of the book.

[65] *Los Angeles Times*, June 30, 1974.

[66] *India News*, Washington, D.C., June 12, 1974.

[67] J. P. Chawla, "Nuclearisation," *Seminar*, October 1971, p. 26.

[68] *Indian News*, June 7, 1974. American experts have challenged this low cost estimate.

[69] *Newsweek*, interview, *op. cit.*

[70] *India News*, Washington, D.C., June 7, 1974.

[71] *Los Angeles Times*, December 1, 1973.

3
Political Beliefs, Ideals, and Historical Traditions

Opinion varies as to the philosophical basis of Indian foreign policy. There are those who maintain that the foundations lie in her ancient thinking and heritage.

> Buddha's voice and those of innumerable Hindu prophets also whisper in the ears of modern Indians that nothing is all good or all bad. In India's noninvolvement in the Cold War and in her attitude toward the West and Russia, ancient themes are still at work.[1]

Then there are those who make a strong case that Indian foreign policy has been molded strictly by the ideological orientation of the late Prime Minister Nehru.

> ... the principal source of Indian thinking on the subject of foreign affairs is neither Hinduism, Buddhism, Gandhianism, the Western European tradition, nor a rational analysis of reality in terms of India's long-range national interest, but the complex biography of the Prime Minister.[2]

On the other hand the late prime minister himself, speaking on foreign affairs in the lower house of Parliament on December 9, 1958, said:

> ... It is completely incorrect to call our policy 'Nehru' policy.... I have not originated it. It is a policy inherent in the past thinking of India, inherent in the whole mental outlook of India, inherent in the conditioning of the Indian mind during our struggle for freedom, and inherent in the circumstances of the world today.[3]

Actually, at the time of independence certain thought patterns dominated the Indian mind and influenced the policymakers, which, given the exigencies of the international situation, often led to contradiction and inconsistency so apparent that the policymakers were embarrassed and found themselves ill at ease in justifying their actions.[4] During the period of British domination and the struggle for independence, India's leaders became impressed with certain ideas. These ideas repeatedly found expression in statements on domestic and international politics; and in time they influenced the thoughts and actions of those who took over the reins of government after independence. Indian views on nonviolence, morality in politics, colonialism, racialism and Asian unity merit some attention.

Nonviolence and Morality

Many Indian authors stress the point that the tradition of nonviolence in Indian culture and politics goes far back to the time of Emperor Ashoka, who ruled sometime between 270 B.C. and 230 B.C.

> ... When Ashoka after the experience of devastation caused by the Kalinga war became a Buddhist and gave up conquest and war as instruments of his foreign policy, a new dimension of inter-state relations became possible.... Ashokan edicts and *Suvarnapralihasa* are the greatest manifestos ancient India produced.[5]

For modern India, however, it was Mahatma Gandhi who gave birth to the concept of nonviolence as a weapon to gain political power. It was Gandhi who influenced the thought of Indian masses and free India's rulers.

In order to secure independence from the British, Gandhi wanted a revolution through nonviolent means. For him there existed only one morality, the morality of love. The rulers and the ruled—the colonial masters and those fighting for independence—were all subject to this common morality. Even as Gandhi fought the British, he insisted that the struggle contain no elements of hatred, personal or collective. He coined the phrase, "we hate the sin and not the sinner." For Gandhi suffering was the law of human beings; war was the law of the jungle.

> But suffering is infinitely more powerful than the law of the jungle for converting the opponent and opening his ears, which are otherwise shut, to the voice of reason.... Suffering is the badge of the human race, not the sword. Nonviolence is a power which can be wielded equally by all—children, young men and women or grown up people—provided they have a living faith in the God of Love and have therefore equal love for all mankind.[6]

Stressing that ends and means are inseparable, Gandhi led the national movement to its goal of independence through a series of campaigns of *Satyagraha* or nonviolent noncooperation. Extending this approach to international politics, when at a given point during World War II Japan's invasion of India seemed imminent, he advised the Indian people to prepare for a nonviolent resistance against such an exigency.

When India became free, Gandhi persisted in his call for the use of nonviolence. Learning that the independent government of India under Nehru's leadership in September, 1946, had presented a military budget identical to what it had been under British rule, Gandhi wrote a note of protest to Nehru: "I have told our people not to depend on the military and the police.... You cannot say it is good in one place and bad in another. The military help will degrade you."[7]

While Nehru, as the first prime minister and foreign minister of independent India, pursued policies many of which were in stark contrast to some of the beliefs and appeals of Gandhi, it is apparent that Gandhi's message of nonviolence and emphasis on ethics did not go totally unheeded by the leaders of free India.

Public statements of Congress Party leaders were tinged with a heavy moral tone. Nehru hammered away at the theme that Gandhian ethics played a dominant role in India's foreign policy. In a broadcast to the United States from New Delhi in April, 1948, he expressed his firm belief that Gandhi, in leading India to freedom by nonviolent means, had opened a new avenue to world peace. It would be well for the world, he said, to follow Gandhi's counsel that the human spirit was more powerful than any military machine, and that only nonviolent means could achieve a lasting solution to international disputes.

> We may not, in the world as it is constituted today, even rule out war absolutely. But I have become more and more convinced that so long as we do not recognize the supremacy of the moral law in our national and international relations, we shall have no enduring peace.[8]

As expressed earlier, were an attempt made to show that Nehru's words and actions were always in accord with Gandhian thinking, it would surely fail. As a writer and a speaker Nehru was prolific; therefore, not only can one find a quotation from him on almost any theme or subject, but one can also discover the contradictions. Thus even as he was wedded to a moralistic approach, he said once:

> The strength which limits or, at any rate, conditions the foreign policy of a country may be military, financial or, if I may use the word, moral. It is obvious that India has neither military nor financial strength.[9]

Was there an implication here that if India had the desired military and financial strength she would be less likely to wield the sword of morality? Regardless, accent on spiritual and moral values has always been prominent in Indian attitudes. It surfaced again and again in pre- and postindependence politics.[10]

Anticolonialism and Racialism

Indian attitudes on colonialism and imperialism are deeply rooted. They come more from a national experience than from any philosophical leanings. For even though Indian history goes as far back as 3000 B.C., once the British gained control, there came about in so many ways a complete break with India's past. A new entity called "British India" was born. The forces that ultimately led to the independence of India from the British were mostly a product of that political and economic environment introduced by the British. Remaining under the heel of a foreigner for nearly two centuries was not an easy existence, and the struggle for independence was a long hard-fought battle which at times had very bitter overtones. During this encounter the Indian people, and especially the Indian leaders, suffered certain mental and physical experiences which left an indelible mark on their memory. Thus was born a deep aversion to colonialism and imperialism.

In his presidential address before the annual session of the Indian National Congress in 1927, Dr. M. A. Ansari said:

> The history of the philanthropic burglary on the part of Europe is written in blood and suffering from Congo to Canton. Once India is free the whole edifice of imperialism will collapse as this is the keystone of the arch of imperialism.[11]

Nehru expressed his feelings about the British rule in a letter to his daughter Indira Gandhi in December, 1932:

> We have been living under a huge machine that has exploited and crushed India's millions. This machine is the machine of the new imperialism, the outcome of industrial capitalism.... They cannot be improved; the only real improvement is to do away with them altogether.[12]

British rule in India gave birth not only to anticolonial attitudes, it also engendered the belief that imperialism was a disease peculiarly characteristic of the Western capitalist countries, and that most of the industrially backward countries of Asia and Africa had fallen prey to the expansionist drive of these Western countries looking for cheap labor, raw materials and markets. Thus imperialism was a phenomenon which had to be fought on a worldwide basis. Once again Nehru's words explain this better than those of any other Indian leader. He wrote:

> Capitalism led also to another and fiercer phase of imperialism.... All over the world there was a fierce scramble for empire. I have already told you in some detail of what happened in Asia, in India, China, farther India and Persia. The European Powers now fell like vultures on Africa, and divided it amongst themselves.... Rudyard Kipling, the popular poet of British imperialism, sang of the 'white man's burdens.' The French talked of the *mission civilisatrice,* the civilizing mission of France. The Germans, of course, had to spread their *Kultur.* So these civilizers and improvers and bearers of other people's burdens went in a spirit of utter sacrifice and sat on the backs of the brown man and the yellow and the black. And nobody sang about the black man's burden.[13]

Opposition to foreign rule was only one among the several trends of thought fostered by British control of India. Another attitude that became fixed in the Indian mind as a result of this experience was antiracialism. For the Indian racialism was the direct consequence of imperialism practiced by the Europeans against the Asians.

Under the British rule in India every European, whether he was German, French, or Belgian, was entitled to certain privileges which marked him as a member of the ruling group. Railway carriages, station retiring rooms, benches in parks, and social clubs were marked: "For Europeans Only." The Indian intelligentsia were highly resentful of these restrictions, especially when they had to suffer this discrimination on their own home ground.

Today, resentment against racial discrimination is openly manifest all over the world, and it is being battled on many fronts. But during the struggle for independence in India, not only did the educated elements of Indian society feel that they were alone in fighting racial discrimination but they also believed that their awareness of this sad state was far more acute. Thus racial discrimination cut deep into the Indian soul and was an extremely sensitive issue. Wrote Nehru:

> Biologists tell us that racialism is a myth and that there is no such thing as a master race. But we in India have known racialism in all its forms ever since the commencement of British rule ... it is better that both Indians and Englishmen should know it for that is the psychological

background of England's connection with India, and psychology counts and racial memories are long.[14]

Having suffered the phenomenon at home, the Indian leaders considered it their duty after independence to oppose racialism on the international scene. A natural outcome was that the feelings of resentment against colonialism and racialism gave an anti-Western stance to Indian foreign policy pronouncements. India used every occasion in the United Nations and outside to announce that no more would the dominance of Europe and America, either culturally or politically, be tolerated silently.

In this context India found membership in the United Nations rewarding, if not completely satisfactory. One of the first complaints India brought before the U.N. in 1946 was that of discrimination against people of Indian descent in the Union of South Africa. While the international organization failed to solve the problem, the forum of the U.N. enabled India to spotlight discriminatory practices. The result was that the eyes of the world focused upon this problem. The Asian-African countries united on this issue and saw it as a test case for measuring the sincerity of the Western democracies on the matter of freedom and equality.

In her attempts to root out colonialism through the channels of the U.N., India succeeded in applying continuous pressure against those countries that still held colonies in parts of Asia and Africa, in the immediate post-World War II period. India's attempts to assist Indonesia in gaining independence with the help of the United Nations were successful. And while India and the like-minded nations did not succeed in bringing about U.N. intervention in Tunisia and Morocco, their success in having the General Assembly debate the issues apparently was a factor in the French effort to seek a solution to these problems.

India carried her fight against colonialism to another front in the U.N. Through the General Assembly and the Trusteeship Council, she sought adoption of measures which would enable the U.N. to assist the people of trust territories to gain self-government as early as possible. While India ran headlong into opposition from members such as Britain and France, who were in charge of administering many trust areas at the time, India found this channel a useful one to embarrass the Western colonial powers and to attack the practice of colonialism.

Asianism

Immediately after independence, India made great efforts to weave a closer bond between herself and the other countries of Asia. Tagore, in relating his impressions about his visit to China in 1924, expresses well the sentiments Indian leaders held toward Asia and the Asians prior to independence. In his narrative, Tagore says that he experienced a very strong feeling of kinship toward the Chinese, despite the fact that they are very different from the Indians in physical features as well as cultural background. He goes on to say that ". . . the relationship between China and India was built not through the infliction of suffering, but through the acceptance of sacrifice, and our countries were united through that truth which enables us to feel those who are distant and different to be near and meaningful to us."[15]

However, India's Asianism, which was greatly emphasized in the twentieth century, was more a by-product of her anticolonial and antiracial feelings than anything else. A link based on past cultural contacts was there, but it was the realization of the shared experience of foreign rule that generated sympathy and an urge for unity.

All through the twentieth century until the eve of World War II, every state in Asia except for Japan was under European control in some form or another. Comparatively speaking the status of India, Burma, Ceylon, Indonesia, Indochina, Malaya and the Philippines was that of colonies. But even the states of China, Nepal, and Thailand were independent in name only. They were subject to intense economic and political pressure from foreign European powers, and in the case of China she was also a victim of Japanese imperialism.

No wonder then that when the League of Nations came into being after World War I, leaders of national movements in Asia saw it as a tool of Western Europe conceived with the purpose of maintaining the status quo on the world scene. And so the Asian delegates to the International Conference for World Peace, held at Bierville, France, in 1926, submitted a memorandum to the Conference which said:

> Establish a brotherhood of cooperation between Asia and Europe, and you would have taken the biggest step towards peace. What is it that stands in the way of such a cooperation? It is the union of European Powers for the exploitation of Asia and for the subordination of new peoples. . . . In Asia, it is not the Englishman, or the Frenchman, or the Dutchman, but the Europeans against the Asiatics that exists.[16]

It was with this background in mind that Sardar Vallabhbhai Patel, free India's first home minister and deputy prime minister, inaugurating a new Indonesian Service by All India Radio, New Delhi in October, 1947, spoke of India's ancient cultural ties with Indonesia and pledged that India would work for Indonesia's freedom relentlessly. He said:

After years of heroic struggles, India has attained her full independence. Indonesia is still in the grip of foreign rule.... India knows that there can be no real freedom for her so long as there are manacles round Indonesia's wrists. We, therefore, send to you, Indonesians, the most sincere assurance of our support in your struggle for emancipation.[17]

There was a gradual retreat of European powers from most of Asia, not by any means voluntarily in every case, soon after the end of World War II. And while states of Asia as independent entities did not manifest any overwhelming desire to present a united front, free India's leaders continued to voice their wish for Asian harmony and solidarity. Once free, India saw herself as the natural leader to uproot European influence from Asia completely, and to encourage Asian cooperation on the economic and the strategic fronts.

The idea of India's leadership in Asia was not new in itself. As early as 1918, there was talk of an Asian Federation with India as the pivot. Mahatma Gandhi maintained that India was the key to the exploitation of Asiatic peoples and when India became independent Western powers would be unable to keep their hold on other Asian countries.[18] Once India became independent, however, this concept of considering her as the hub of political and economic activity in Asia gained credence.

On Nehru's initiative, India sponsored the Asian Relations Conference which was held in New Delhi during March, 1947. Representatives of twenty-eight Asian countries gathered together. The meeting, first of its kind, was on an unofficial footing: No resolutions were passed, no political questions were discussed, and the agenda was free from controversial matters. Nehru's address to the Conference showed that while he was trying to speak to the rest of the world as the "voice of Asia," he was at the same time urging his fellow Asians to follow a common policy which was primarily in their interest, independent, and Asian in origin. He talked of the vital role that was Asia's in a world of crisis and he observed that Asian countries would play this role free from dictates of others.[19]

This was the beginning of India's efforts to make her weight felt in Asian affairs. When Nehru visited the United Nations in Paris in November, 1948, the Indian delegation organized a meeting of the Asian delegates to encourage prior consultation among themselves on the various issues before the U.N.

A very important move was made when India called a conference of the Asian nations to consider the case of Dutch aggression in Indonesia. On January 20, 1949, delegates from nineteen nations met in New Delhi to frame and submit proposals to the Security Council on the restoration of peace and freedom to Indonesia, and to devise machinery and procedures by which the represented governments could keep in touch with one another for consultation and concerted action.

If the Conference accomplished nothing else, it certainly succeeded in drawing the attention of the world to the urgency of the Indonesian case. It also brought about cooperation in the U.N. on the part of the countries that had gathered in New Delhi. Ultimately, this action helped to accelerate a quick settlement between Indonesia and the Netherlands.

More significantly it provided the limelight for India who was quick to seize upon an opportunity to display her keen interest in Asian affairs. It was one more chance for Nehru to give warning that interference in Asian affairs could no longer go unchallenged. As he put it at the Conference:

> ... If this gathering is significant today, it is still more significant in the perspective of tomorrow. Asia, too long submissive and dependent and a plaything of other countries, will no longer brook any interference with her freedom.[20]

Foreign policies of mainland China under the leadership of the Communist regime, cold war tactics of the superpowers, prolonged involvement of the United States in the Vietnam war, ceaseless tensions between India and Pakistan, and other related developments unleashed forces which not only brought an end to India's noticeable influence in Asia, but also put a damper on the creation of a common Asian approach to international situations. Nevertheless, during the first decade after independence, India's leadership did everything to display its pro-Asian bias, even though in the long run the policy registered little positive gain.

Notes

[1]Chester Bowles, *Ambassador's Report* (New York: Harper and Brothers, 1954), p. 46

[2]Adda B. Bozeman, "India's Foreign Policy Today," *World Politics*, Vol. 10, No. 2 (Jan., 1958), p. 273.

[3]Jawaharlal Nehru, *India's Foreign Policy* (New Delhi: The Publications Division, Ministry of Information and Broadcasting), p. 80.

[4]India's stand on the Tibetan crisis in 1950, and the Egyptian and Hungarian crisis in 1956 highlights this dilemma.

[5]K. Satchidananda Murty, "India's Foreign Policy: Ideological Moorings," in K. P. Misra (Ed.), *Studies in Indian Foreign Policy* (Delhi: Vikas Publications, 1969), pp. 18–19.

[6]Mahatma Gandhi, as quoted in *All Men Are Brothers*, published by UNESCO, (New York: Columbia University Press, 1958), p. 91.

[7]D. G. Tendulkar, *Mahatma*, Vol. 7, 1945–47, p. 334. When war broke out between India and Pakistan over the Kashmir dispute in 1947, it is

interesting to note that Gandhi advised Nehru against the use of military force. "India, according to Gandhi, might easily have offered Kashmir non-violent aid, and if the defenders did not surrender, but died at their posts without hatred for the attackers, this would have been a heroic deed, in which India would have played some small part, and which could have lent meaning to the Kashmir dispute for the whole world." This account is given by Arne Naess in *Gandhi and the Nuclear Age* (New Jersey: The Bedminster Press, 1965), p. 110.

[8] Jawahrlal Nehru, *Independence and After* (New York: The John Day Company, 1950), pp. 302–303

[9] *Jawaharlal Nehru's Speeches 1949–1953* (New Delhi: The Publications Division, Government of India, 1954), p. 230.

[10] Bandyopadhyaya, once a foreign service officer in the Ministry of External Affairs, states in his book, *The Making of India's Foreign Policy*, that Nehru's idealism prevented India from organizing an effective intelligence gathering agency and that this was in tune with "India's idealist political tradition and the broad objectives and principles of India's foreign policy, all of which have been opposed to the clandestine and manipulative approach to international politics." Herbert C Friedmann in an article "Politics and Mind-A Contrast Between India and the West," *Indian Year Book of International Affairs*, Vol. II (Madras, 1952), suggests that "power politics is strictly connected with certain aspects of the Western attitudes of mind, which are to some extent foreign to Indian."

[11] Quoted by Har Govind Pant in *India's Foreign Policy* (Jaipur: Panchsheel Prakashan, 1971), p. 3.

[12] Jawaharlal Nehru, *Glimpses of World History* (London: Lindsay Drummond Limited, 1939), p. 429.

[13] *Ibid.*, pp. 554–60

[14] Jawaharalal Nehru, *The Discovery of India* (Calcutta: The Signet Press, 1946), pp. 386–87.

[15] Amiya Chakravarty (ed.), *A Tagore Reader* (Boston: Beacon Press, 1966), p. 198. Rabindra Nath Tagore (1861–1941), is without question recognized as modern India's literary genius.

[16] K. M. Pannikar, "Asia and Peace," cited by K. P. Karunakaran in *India in World Affairs* (London: Oxford University Press, 1952), pp. 64–65.

[17] *Speeches of Sardar Patel 1947–1950* (New Delhi: Publications Division, Ministry of Information and Broadcasting Government of India, 1967), p. 173.

[18] Werner Levi, *Free India in Asia* (Minneapolis: University of Minnesota Press, 1952), pp. 31–33.

[19] *Independence and After*, op. cit., p. 298.

[20] *Ibid.*, p. 333.

4

Foreign Policy Formulation

It is not possible to state categorically who makes foreign policy in a given country. One can come close to pinning down the ultimate decision makers in a dictatorial system of government. But in a democratic society governed by a constitution, not only does one have to account for the influence exercised by the formal institutions and agencies created by the fundamental law of the land, but one has also to search below the formal structures. The informal practices that develop in time place the real power of foreign policymaking in the hands of individuals who might—and then again might not—be a part of the formal structure. Under these circumstances, in the case of a democratic country like India, all one can do is to identify the institutions and the individuals that participate in the foreign policy decisions, and assess the degree of impact each has on the final decisions.

Role of the Prime Minister as Leader

During his lifetime, the conduct and content of independent India's foreign policy were largely dictated by Nehru. Aside from the fact that he occupied the offices of prime minister and foreign minister from 1947 to 1964, the small segment of the Indian population which is interested in foreign policy displayed total confidence in his knowledge of external affairs and his ability to deal with foreign governments and diplomats. Voices of doubt and dissent were raised in 1962 after the Chinese invasion, but even then his foreign policy-making powers were not questioned seriously in party or parliament. On the one hand this faith in Nehru's capability to make effective foreign policy was founded in the quick rise of India's prestige on the international scene soon after independence; on the other hand it was accepted as a fact within the ruling party and among the articulate segments of the public that Nehru's background in foreign affairs was unmatched by any other leader.

The Indian National Congress Party showed a serious concern for foreign affairs for the first time in 1920, and it was Nehru who took the greatest interest and initiative. Nehru represented his party at the meeting of the International Congress against Imperialism held at Brussels in February 1927. In one of his addresses to the conference he maintained that the Indian National Congress "is based on the most intense internationalism." Considering the time at which this statement was made, it was more an expression of Nehru's own thinking than that of the party leadership, who were totally immersed in the national movement for self-rule. When Nehru returned from the Brussels conference his enthusiasm for international politics was clearly in evidence in the many proposals he placed before the Indian National Congress in December 1927; almost all of them dealt with foreign policy matters. From then on Nehru assumed the role of the Congress spokesman in international affairs. It was under his guidance that the party set up its own Foreign Department in 1928 to continue and further the contacts he had made with many of the Asian and African leaders at Brussels. It was, therefore, no surprise that during the transitional period when the British were preparing for transfer of power to Indian hands, Nehru was appointed as member for external affairs in the Interim government in 1946.

When India achieved the status of a sovereign state, it followed naturally that Nehru became responsible for formulating, expounding, and even implementing Indian foreign policy. "If Nehru was given carte blanche in foreign policy, it was, after all, his portfolio; more than that, they [members of the cabinet] knew little about it and felt it was in competent hands, at least until the last year and a half."[1]

The extent to which Nehru was the sole architect of Indian foreign policy is well-illustrated by an incident related by K. P. S.

Menon, one-time foreign secretary to the Government of India. According to Menon's account, when the United States invited India to participate in the San Francisco Conference to draft a peace treaty for Japan, Nehru opposed the idea. He stuck to his position even when it was suggested that India's refusal would be deeply resented by the United States. Nehru was of the opinion that it would be better for India to sign a separate peace treaty with Japan containing no clause which the Japanese government might consider obnoxious. India's chargé d'affaires in Washington, D.C. was asked to communicate India's stand on the matter to John Foster Dulles. Menon states that Dulles displayed extreme anger when informed of this, and was almost rude to the Indian diplomat. When Nehru learned of this, not only did he adhere to his original position but personally drafted a very strong letter to the U.S. government thus bringing the episode to an end.[2]

The extent to which Nehru dictated even the last detail of a foreign policy decision is highlighted by another account.

The United Nations, in bringing the Korean War to an end in 1953, created the Neutral Nations Repatriation Commission (NNRC) to determine the fate of prisoners on both sides. Lt. Gen. K. S. Thimayya was chosen by India to represent her as chairman of the NNRC. Lt. Gen. B. M. Kaul was nominated by Thimayya as his chief of staff. Just before Kaul was ready to leave for Korea, Nehru sent for him and proceeded to explain that in the problem of prisoners of war both the U.S.A. and the USSR would be very anxious to establish the correctness of their ideologies:

> They were bound to exert much pressure on us and it was, Nehru said, essential that we not only observed a strictly impartial attitude but also succeeded in giving an impression of doing so. As Chairman of the Commission, India would occupy a position of trust and must create a stabilizing atmosphere of impartiality around ourselves in this combustible situation and thus reduce the tension which existed internationally. He suggested we make an initial gesture by sending a message of goodwill to all prisoners. We should try and learn the Korean language as it would give the impression of our interestedness in their problems. He said there might be some prisoners not willing to go home; we should, therefore, start with a batch appearing to be willing to do so. He felt that as most prisoners were ordinary peasants, free from politics, and hence naturally anxious to get back home, we should treat them sympathetically. He suggested we should segregate prisoners who were objectionable and watch for their ring leaders. We might find them reluctant to give details of their antecedents to the interrogators. They should, in that case, be persuaded to do so. Nehru finally said if there was a deadlock in any situation, we should try and solve it informally. As regarding China, he said we were friendly with that country, as we were with others, and shared a long border with her. It would be unwise on our part, therefore, to antagonize a friendly neighbor unnecessarily.

> We should, in any case, take no sides but bear in mind our national policies.[3]

No head of government after Nehru has quite equaled the role he played in directing India's foreign affairs. But in a country where international politics was the concern of a very limited few until independence in 1947, despite India's feverish activity in the world arena during the last twenty years, the number of individuals and groups who participate in foreign policymaking remains sparse. The result is that the head of the government as the leader of the country continues to have a dominant influence in the nation's foreign policy orientation.

Lal Bahadur Shastri, who succeeded Nehru as prime minister from June 1964 to January 1966, could not claim Nehru's expertise in foreign affairs. Nonetheless, following the pattern set by Nehru, Shastri took over the portfolio of external affairs in addition to assuming the prime ministership. Although he did not continue to hold both these offices throughout his brief two year incumbency, the role of the leader in foreign policymaking does not appear to have diminished to any significant degree while the reins of government were in his hands. In announcing India's stand on the atom bomb and nuclear nonproliferation treaty, he did not hesitate to state publicly that the matter had not been discussed by the Cabinet. At the Cairo Conference of nonaligned nations in October, 1964, Shastri proposed that in view of China's reported intention of exploding a nuclear bomb, a special mission should be dispatched to persuade her that she should not develop nuclear weapons. Seemingly Shastri initiated the proposal on his own without prior discussion at any level as to the fruitfulness or futility of such a gesture.[4]

Mrs. Indira Gandhi succeeded Shastri as India's prime minister in January, 1966. She has included a minister for external affairs in her Cabinet from the start, except for the period between 1967 and 1969 when she took over the External Affairs portfolio herself. But those close to the seat of power maintain that like her father, Prime Minister Gandhi is often given to making foreign policy decisions without consulting the Cabinet or any other source. During Shastri's regime the prime minister began to seek advice for directing foreign affairs, and since then the predominance exercised by the leader over the conduct of foreign policy has somewhat diminished. Nevertheless, in India as in other states, foreign policy is a subject of interest for only a small segment of the population. The largest number of these generally support the broad principles of Indian foreign policy as espoused by the government in power. While groups and individuals other than those in power do freely articulate their views on foreign policy issues, their impact on specific decisions is indeed minimal.

Role of the Cabinet

The Constitution of India places all executive power in the hands of the president. It also provides for a council of ministers headed by a prime minister to "aid and advise the president in the exercise of his functions." The president appoints the prime minister, who in turn advises the president as to the other appointments within the council of ministers, or the Indian Cabinet. Practice has established two things. Firstly, the president has emerged as the ceremonial head of state. Executive power in reality is exercised by the prime minister and his or her Cabinet. Secondly, the leader of the party which commands a majority in the Lok Sabha (lower house of the Indian Parliament) is always appointed as the prime minister.

According to the Constitution, ministers must hold seats in the Parliament either at the time of appointment or within six months of their appointment. They hold office at the pleasure of the president, but collectively the Cabinet is responsible to the Lok Sabha. The Cabinet functions on the principle of joint responsibility and remains in office as long as it enjoys the confidence of the lower house of the Parliament. If it fails to secure a majority vote on a major issue, the Cabinet must resign. The president then has the liberty to appoint another Cabinet which he feels would command a majority, or he can on the advice of the prime minister dissolve the lower house and call for new elections.

In theory, like Cabinet systems of government in general, the Indian Cabinet is expected to formulate the government's legislative program as a whole, and administer it. No individual minister can express disagreement with Cabinet policy in public. If he has strong objections to such policy, he must resign to state his opposition in the open. But as Krishna Menon, at one time defense minister of India, tells us:

> In a parliamentary system of government, by which I mean practically all governments in the Commonwealth, the way a Cabinet functions and the number of its meetings is very largely ad hoc, informal, flexible. There are no set rules, no voting, not even a strict adherence to an agenda. Whatever is done is mostly done merely for functional reasons. In any Cabinet the practice would vary according to its age, the time during which its members have sat in it without change, the period during which its principal person, the prime minister, has presided over it, and so on. A kind of gearing-in takes place and its own conventions get set up and its own disregard for conventions also becomes a convention.[5]

Krishna Menon in his statements suggests further that in the Indian Cabinet the prime minister expects and receives a somewhat "reverential" response from his colleagues. The prime minister does not discuss all matters with the Cabinet at large. There is no regular schedule of meetings or agenda for the Cabinet. Whatever the agenda, it has to receive advance approval of the prime minister. Most of the decisions are made outside the Cabinet, and in making these decisions the prime minister consults only with those who are intimately concerned with a particular issue, or those few who are close to him and enjoy his confidence. Because of the central role played by finance in almost every issue of substance, however, the finance minister is possibly consulted most often. This does not prevent members of the Cabinet from bringing up matters for deliberation in Cabinet meetings which might or might not be associated with their departments. But a general discussion of any subject does not mean that the Cabinet policy is made by a majority vote or consensus. By and large if a minister governing a department secures the consent of the prime minister on a certain issue, he expects that the prime minister will carry the rest of the Cabinet behind him. We also learn from Krishna Menon that akin to the British pattern, India's prime minister holds special responsibilities for foreign affairs and defense.[6] Thus while matters of foreign policy and defense do crop up for general discussion in the Cabinet from time to time, the influence it exerts on foreign policymaking is rather minor.

During the 1950s Prime Minister Nehru created a number of Cabinet committees, including the Defense Committee and the Foreign Affairs Committee. Now considered defunct, their membership varied with each prime minister. Moreover, the role they played in decision making has also undergone change over a period of years.

The Defense Committee of the Cabinet and the Foreign Affairs Committee were formidable until sometime around 1962. The prime minister, always the chairman, handpicked the other members of the committees. In addition to the prime minister, the three or four other members who served from time to time were men like Krishna Menon, Maulana Azad, Pandit Pant, Rafi Ahmed Kidwai, T. T. Krishnamachari, and a few others who were senior colleagues of Nehru or were people in whom he placed special trust. Unlike other committees of the Cabinet, the decisions of the Defense Committee and the Foreign Affairs Committee were treated as Cabinet decisions. After the Sino-Indian confrontation in 1962, however, Nehru established the Emergency Committee of the Cabinet. Also referred to as the "inner cabinet," it was composed of the prime minister, home minister, external affairs minister, defense minister, and the finance minister. The sixth place on the committee was not a fixed one and went to the minister whose advice or role the prime minister in power considered crucial. The Emergency Committee of the Cabinet supplanted the Defense and Foreign Affairs committees, and served as the key organ in discussing and formulating foreign and defense policy. In the late sixties Mrs. Gandhi created the Political Affairs Committee. Its composition is essentially the same as that of the Emergency Committee. With all the other committees abolished, the Political Affairs Committee has now taken over the tasks previously assigned to the others.

Despite all signs that the Cabinet as a whole plays an insignificant part in foreign policy formulation, Cabinet ministers have on occasion been in strong enough disagreement with their prime minister on foreign policy that they have felt compelled to resign. S. P. Mookerjee, the minister of industry and supply, and K. C. Neogy, the commerce minister, resigned in 1950 in opposition to the agreement made by the prime ministers of India and Pakistan to ease religious tensions caused by problems of migration between India and Pakistan. Commerce Minister T. T. Krishnamachari resigned in early 1955 over Soviet steel negotiations. Mahavir Tyagi, the rehabilitation minister, resigned in January, 1966, in opposition to the Tashkent Pact agreed upon by Prime Minister Shastri and President Ayub to bring an end to hostilities over Kashmir. Ashok Mehta, minister for planning and social welfare, resigned from Mrs. Gandhi's Cabinet in 1968, maintaining that she had not taken a strong enough stand against the Soviet invasion of Czechoslovakia. These examples indicate that Cabinet members who do not participate in the initial decision making in the area of external affairs do, nevertheless, feel free to express their differences in Cabinet meetings. However, they must resign to express their opinions publicly.

Role of the Parliament

The Constitution of India grants the Parliament exclusive power to make laws in respect to foreign affairs, and all matters which bring the Union into relation with any foreign country. But an examination of the composition of the Indian Parliament reveals that while the Parliament, especially the powerful lower house, truly represents the overwhelming rural character of the Indian society as a whole, it also reflects that the largest number of Parliament members have no familiarity or concern with forcign policy issues. The Lok Sabhas (lower house of parliament) have conformed more and more to the overall social structure of the people. The basic distinction in the social structure of the Indian population is that between the rural and the urban. Rural interests have gained the upper hand during the years since independence.

> In this sense the Lok Sabha today is a more representative body than its predecessors of the past and pre-Independence periods. Parliament is

being moulded increasingly in the nation's image. Yet it is true, and this is perhaps the major anomaly of political life in India, that the center of power, that is to say the cabinet and the ministry, continues to be dominated by nonrural, professional groups.[7]

The presence of comfortable Congress Party majorities in the Parliament has also created the situation whereby the provisions of the Constitution have not barred but assisted the government in having a comparatively free hand in shaping foreign policy. The treaty-making powers of the executive branch serve as one example of the passivity with which the Parliament has accepted executive supremacy in the field of foreign affairs. None of the treaties which the Indian Republic has entered into with other countries thus far have been submitted to the Parliament for approval. In pronouncing judgment on a case the Calcutta High Court held: "Making a treaty is an executive act and not a legislative act.... The president makes a treaty in exercise of his executive power and no court of law in India can question its validity."[8] The Government of India informed the United Nations through a memorandum to the Secretary General in 1951 that, "... the president's power to enter into treaties remains unfettered by any 'internal restrictions.' "[9]

Few of the ruling party members take an active part in debates on the floor of the House. Rarely do those who speak express opinions which are at variance with official government policy. Faithful to parliamentary tradition, members of the opposition parties in Parliament employ every technique and opportunity open to them to check and possibly influence the foreign policy decisions of the government. But their effectiveness is quite limited; firstly because they lack the voting strength, and secondly because the opposition is badly split from within.

In general elections based on universal adult suffrage held in India in 1951–52, 1957 and 1962, out of a total of approximately 500 seats in the lower house of Parliament, the ruling Congress Party won 364, 371 and 361 seats respectively. The combined strength of all opposition parties ranged from 129 to 139 seats in the general elections. Furthermore, the opposition was represented by as many as fifteen to twenty parties. General elections in 1967 shattered the overwhelming dominance of the Congress Party. It won only 282 seats out of a total of 518 seats.[10] While many opposition parties gained at the cost of the Congress, by itself not one of them received even as many as the 50 seats which would have qualified it as the "legal opposition." The Indian Constitution provides that if a party comes to occupy ten percent of the total membership of the Lok Sabha, it is labeled the "legally constituted opposition," and among other privileges receives the courtesy of regular consultation by the government in power. So far no party in the Indian Parliament has won enough seats to be thus recognized. Out of ten major opposition parties represented in the Lok Sabha in 1967, only the Swatantra and Jan Sangh Party came close to gaining "opposition" status with 42 and 35 seats respectively. The task of the opposition is made even more difficult by the fact that foreign policy views of parties like the Socialist Party, the Communist Party, the Swatantra Party, the Jan Sangh Party, and the Independents are poles apart.

> The Opposition in India is not articulated. In the Indian Parliament as many as three types of opposition exist. There is the vigorous opposition from the extreme left consisting of the Communists and other Marxist sections.... In recent times, of course, there have been grounds of agreement between the Congress and the Communists, particularly in matters of foreign policy, because of the increasing friendly relations between India and the USSR.... There are, then, the Praja Socialists whose criticisms are usually milder as their programs often do not concretely differ from those of the Congress and as they believe in the desirability and practicality of the parliamentary democratic method for bringing about the desired social and economic changes in India. There is, lastly, the opposition from the Jan Sangh, the Hindu Mahasabha, and others, which draw inspiration from the glorious Indian tradition, dislike radical social and economic reforms, stand for a United India, and advocate a tough policy towards Pakistan. This is the heterogeneous, unintegrated opposition that functions in the parliamentary government in India today ... the Opposition has been shorn of much of its effective powers which it could have exercised against the ruling authority in the parliament had it been homogeneous, at least united.[11]

The Indian Parliament has a Consultative Committee on Foreign Affairs. At the beginning of each new Parliament, the Chief Government Whip asks the various political parties represented in the two houses of Parliament to name a candidate for membership on the Committee. These party nominees, the foreign minister and the minister of state for external affairs constitute the Committee. It is expected to meet at least twice during each session of the Parliament. Its primary function is to advise the foreign minister on policy problems. To date the Committee has neither met regularly, nor played an advisory role in foreign policymaking. The foreign minister has called the Committee into session on special occasions only to inform members about official policy line on certain issues. When asked about the importance of the committee, the late Krishna Menon replied: "I don't know because, as a minister, I found it was more akin to a conference! Unfortunately, a few people tended to monopolize the time. You give information but are more or less forced into the position of being on the defensive ... if a minister wants something carried it's a useful instrument."[12] According to one-time foreign minister, M. C. Chagla, the committee is "more of an agency for getting policies accepted and meeting criticism than for influencing foreign policy."[13]

Parliament does provide, however, an important public forum for those who disagree with the official line in foreign policy issues. Question hour, five days in the lower house and four days in the upper house, assures the dissident members an opportunity to interrogate the government benches about matters relating to foreign policy decisions. Twice a week, a half hour is allotted for holding discussions on matters of national importance. The account of Parliament's proceedings shows that each year there are at least six or seven full-blown debates on foreign affairs in the Indian Parliament in which the Opposition participates with no holds barred. There also have been occasions when parliamentary inquiry has led to the surfacing of information which not only embarrassed the government but resulted, in some cases, in a change of policy direction. The Voice of America incident of 1963 is a good example of this.

After the Chinese attack on India in October, 1962, the Government of India decided to purchase abroad a one-megawatt radio transmitter to counter Chinese propaganda in Southeast Asia and Africa. In March, 1963, the "Voice of America" put forward the possibility of negotiating an agreement that would enable India to install the desired transmitter under certain conditions. India's minister of information and broadcasting and the American ambassador to India reached an agreement on July 9, 1963, providing that in return for U.S. delivery of the needed transmitter, India would permit the "Voice of America" to share the transmitter for three hours a day for its broadcasts to Southeast Asia, in addition to the purchase price in rupees. India was to use the rest of the twenty-one hours for her own broadcasts. While Prime Minister Nehru was kept informed about the negotiations and the final agreement, and approved of it, he did not consult or inform the Cabinet about the matter; nor does it appear that he was himself fully aware of the wide implications of the agreement.[14]

The transaction was brought to light for the first time when the Indian press gave publicity to the matter shortly after the signing of the agreement. Press reaction was highly critical of the government policy. The opposition parties carried the issue to the floor of the Parliament on the very first day it opened after the summer recess.

On August 13, 1963, seven motions of no confidence in the government were presented to the speaker of Lok Sabha. During the debate that followed the entire foreign policy of the government was attacked by the Opposition members, but special hostility was displayed against the Indo-U.S. agreement for it was alleged that it destroyed India's nonalignment posture. Even some of the Congress members felt obliged to join the Opposition on this occasion in sharply criticizing the government's conduct.

In outlining the background to the agreement before the lower house on August 14, Prime Minister Nehru took great pains to explain that during the previous few weeks it had become clear that the arrangement made was not in consonance with India's general policy, and steps were being taken to discuss the matter with the U.S. government.

In a foreign affairs debate before the Rajya Sabha (the upper house of the Indian Parliament) on September 3, Nehru admitted that he did not realize the implications of the agreement before it was signed by the Indian Broadcasting Ministry and the United States Information Agency. He declared: "If it cannot be revised radically, we shall do without it."[15]

Following U.S. resistance to Indian efforts to modify the agreement,[16] Mrs. Lakshmani Menon, minister of state for external affairs, announced on November 18, 1963, that the Government of India had notified the U.S. authorities that the agreement could only survive if "there should be no broadcasts from the transmitter by the 'Voice of America.'" Prime Minister Nehru stated on the same day that the agreement was inoperative. Satya Narayan Sinha, minister for information and broadcasting, in answer to a question on the transmitter deal, stated in the Rajya Sabha on February 11, 1964, that "the chapter is almost closed."

Undoubtedly the incident highlights multiple facets of foreign policymaking in India. It does throw considerable light on the role of the Parliament and confirms the views of Krishna Menon in this regard:

> ... Parliament has an educative impact. In my opinion discussions in Parliament have the result of showing the world what we think and that we do think. On the other hand, it shows the limitations of our position since Parliament is often dealing with a fait accompli. This is not peculiar to India although there are certain differences here. I think it performs a very useful function. There are speeches made. Some of the speeches made are a kind of routine opposition and often strong views are expressed. This enables the Prime Minister and Government to feel that even if a thing has to be done for diplomatic or other reasons, Parliament should at least be told about it. Sometimes this may mean that the wise thing cannot be done or has to be delayed—but this is so in all politics. ... Nehru's attitude to Parliament was one of great respect ... I cannot say that the contribution of Parliament in foreign affairs has not been valuable.[17]

Ministry of External Affairs

According to the Rules of Business of the Government of India, foreign affairs are assigned to the Ministry of External Affairs. At the head of the Ministry of External Affairs is the foreign minister. While Nehru held the portfolio of External Affairs himself throughout the period that he was the prime minister, his successor Shastri had followed this practice only for a short time when illness compelled him to transfer the responsibility to another member of his cabinet. Since then, except for a short break, there has been a foreign affairs minister separate from the prime minister.

The minister of external affairs is joined in his task at the "political level" by a deputy minister and three Parliamentary secretaries who maintain liaison with the Parliament but who are not members of the government. Below this level is a body of civil servants who are responsible to the foreign minister. Until 1964 the senior career official was the secretary-general who assisted and advised the minister of external affairs on all important matters of foreign policy.[18] The post of the secretary general was abolished in 1964. The administrative head of the foreign office since then has been the foreign secretary. He is assisted by four under-secretaries, who supervise the twenty-one various divisions of the Ministry.

Prior to independence there was no such thing as the Indian Foreign Service, so to meet the immediate needs of independent India in 1946–47 Prime Minister Nehru recruited a number of capable men who had gained experience in the Indian Civil Service under the British. They formed the nucleus of the Ministry of External Affairs. Further additions were made to this group by drawing talent from the armed forces, business, and the professions on the basis of recommendations made by a Special Selection Board set up for this purpose. Recruitment to the India Foreign Service, subsequent to 1949, has been made by the Union Public Service Commission through a competitive examination which is open to all university graduates between the ages of 21 and 24.

It appears, therefore, that at the beginning the number of civil service officials who manned the important positions in the External Affairs Ministry was small. Then again because most of them had previous association with the colonial regime of the British, a psychological barrier prevented them from becoming too close to the new government or being confident that their advice would be heeded or considered valuable without question. Additionally, of course, the personality and knowledge of India's first foreign minister, Nehru, overwhelmed the External Affairs Ministry.

The pattern of influence exercised by the career officials of the External Affairs Ministry on India's foreign policy during Nehru's tenure as prime minister and foreign minister can be best characterized in these terms: India's foreign policy owed "its inspiration to the intuition of one man. Jawaharlal Nehru." He left its day-to-day operations to the permanent officials of the foreign office, and consulted them on important matters, but as a whole their role was a subordinate one.[19]

Indications are that Nehru's death was followed by greater decision making participation on the part of the permanent civil service officials. Shastri's creation of the Prime Minister's Secretariat in July, 1964, was consequential in placing a significant amount of influence in the hands of the prime minister's secretary. While according to L. K. Jha, secretary to P. M. Shastri, his task was "to prepare drafts of important speeches, statements, and letters," he also admitted that he was consulted by the prime minister regularly on major policy decisions.[20]

Prime Minister Shastri also took some other initiatives. In June, 1965, he appointed a committee to review the structure and organization of the Indian Foreign Service. It was expected that the committee would recommend suggestions that would enable the Foreign Service to meet the future needs of Indian foreign policy more effectively. In addition, in July, 1965, the prime minister agreed to appoint a powerful committee consisting of secretaries of External Affairs, Defense, Finance and the Cabinet to deal with the subject of foreign policymaking. Shastri did not live long enough to see the results of these actions. Prime Minister Gandhi, however, did seize on these initiatives and carried them a step further.

The Policy Planning and Review Division was established in the Ministry of External Affairs late in 1966 to prepare papers on foreign policy matters calculated to deal with current and future contingencies. The Division was granted a measure of independence with the hope that the career officers would see this as an opportunity to contribute to foreign policy formulation. Available records appear to suggest that this agency failed to measure up to expectations.[21] But the emergence of a high powered Foreign Policy and Planning Committee in August, 1971, indicates that the Review Division has become more of a resource agency for this new committee.

The Policy Planning Committee was born at a time when India's foreign policy was under great stress. India had just signed a security treaty with the Soviet Union, breaking previous tradition. Tension between India and Pakistan was rapidly rising over the question of Bangladesh, and there were ominous signs that China and the U.S. would support Pakistan in case of an Indo-Pak confrontation. The committee was considered a major innovation in the decision-making process. It was given the sensitive function of rendering judgment on important decisions, open and secret, related to foreign policy, and those domestic policies which would have a bearing on Indian foreign policy. To give it clout, Prime Minister Gandhi appointed D. P. Dhar, one of her closest aids, as the chairman of the committee. In addition to Dhar, others appointed to this committee were the secretary of external affairs, secretary of defense, secretary of foreign trade, cabinet secretary, private secretary to the prime minister, home secretary, and the chief of Indian intelligence.

To date the Policy Planning Committee remains the most formidable group, outside the Cabinet, making an input in foreign policy formulation. Its contribution is difficult to assess at this time. Indications are that its deliberations will have an influence on Indian foreign policy as long as the committee chairman is a close confidant of the prime minister.

India's foreign policymakers realize that there is a close relationship between Indian economic development needs and foreign policy. Until the early 1960s it was common practice for the Ministries of Finance and Trade to deal with these matters. At times these two ministries signed treaties and agreements with foreign governments relating to economic affairs without any consultation with the External Affairs Ministry. This picture has changed radically since 1966.

The Economic and Coordination Division was established in the Ministry of External Affairs in 1961 to handle all international economic questions. It was expected to help in developing a foreign policy in which political and economic issues were closely integrated. While it acted in an advisory capacity, the Division was expanded in 1966 to enable it to play a greater role in the planning of foreign economic policy. Today the Division has primary responsibility in such areas as trade agreements, foreign aid negotiations, air and shipping agreements, and technical assistance agreements. Through this Division, the External Affairs Ministry now exercises control over all foreign economic agreements. Even when an agreement is formally signed by the Ministry of Trade or Finance, it is the Ministry of External Affairs that initiates and finalizes the negotiations with the help of the Economic Division.

This situation pinpoints two things. First, under the current leadership no other ministry is able to compete with the Ministry of External Affairs in the management of foreign relations. Second, the role of the External Affairs Ministry has expanded considerably in the post-Nehru period. Practices introduced by Shastri and expanded upon by Mrs. Gandhi have permitted the upper echelons of the Foreign Service and other Civil Services to now play an important role in shaping Indian foreign policy. Yet the degree to which the career official has penetrated the decision-making group cannot be precisely determined. Evidence suggests that in recent years career officials have increased their access to policymakers, and their influence on foreign policy is growing.[22]

Notes

[1] Michael Brecher, *Nehru's Mantle* (New York: Fredrick A. Praeger, 1966), p. 95.
[2] K. P. S. Menon, "Recollections and Reflections: A Symposium," *The Illustrated Weekly of India*, Bombay, November 15, 1964.
[3] Lt. Gen. B. M. Kaul, *The Untold Story* (New Delhi: Allied Publishers, 1967), pp. 150–151.
[4] This is indicated in the remarks of Krishna Menon in Michael Brecher's *India and World Politics* (New York: Frederick A. Praeger, 1968), pp. 186–87.
[5] Brecher, *India and World Politics*, p. 245.
[6] *Ibid.*, pp. 234–35.
[7] Surindar Suri, "Lok Sabha Analysis," *Seminar*, New Delhi, February 1962, p. 42.
[8] As quoted by K. Narayan Rao in "Parliamentary Approval of Treaties in India," *The Indian Year Book of International Affairs*, Volume IX–X, 1960, p. 23.
[9] *Ibid.*
[10] The number of seats in the Lok Sabha, the lower house of Parliament, has varied from 489 to the present number of 521.
[11] Santosh Kumar Nandy, "Reflections On the Nature and Significance of the Opposition in the Parliamentary Government in India," *The Indian Journal of Political Science*, Volume 19, 1958, page 44. Although this article was written in 1958, and there have been some changes in party alignments and party strength, the comments about the character of opposition in the Indian Parliament remain quite valid. Two factors of significance have emerged since 1958. The Communist Party has been split into two segments, one Moscow oriented and the other Peking oriented, since the Chinese attack on India in 1962. Also, a new party by the name of Swatantra Party was born in August 1959. It contested elections in 1962 for the first time and has shown popular support in the last two elections. The party represents conservative forces in the country. It supports a private enterprise-based economy as opposed to a state enterprise-based economy. It also opposes the Congress Party's policy of nonalignment and would encourage India's entry into some sort of a military-alliance to boost India's defensive posture vis-à-vis China and Pakistan. Nevertheless, these two developments have not affected the character of the Opposition in the Indian Parliament.
[12] As quoted by Brecher, *India and World Politics*, pp. 264–65.
[13] As quoted by J. Bandyopadhyaya, *The Making of India's Foreign Policy* (New Delhi: Allied Publishers, 1970), p. 135.
[14] *India Parliamentary Lok Sabha Debates*, Volumes 19–20, pp. 1226–1290.
[15] *New York Times*, September 4, 1963.
[16] Ambassador Bowles is alleged to have cautioned India that were she to revise or terminate the agreement, the U.S. Congress might retaliate by turning down the foreign aid to India which was at the time before the House of Representatives for approval.
[17] Brecher, *India and World Politics*, p. 263.
[18] Because the prime minister himself carried the portfolio of foreign affairs between 1947 and 1964, the post of the secretary general held great significance. During this period the secretary general had direct access to

the prime minister and was his primary advisor on details related to foreign policy matters.

[19]Both K.P.S. Menon and Krishna Menon confirm this viewpoint.

[20]For a detailed account, see Brecher, *Nehru's Mantle*, pp. 115–20.

[21]A political commentator on the Indian scene, J. D. Sethi, is of the opinion that PPRD failed to make any positive contribution because it became mired in bureaucratic politics. *The Sunday Statesman* (New Delhi), November 14, 1971.

[22]Swaran Singh and M. C. Chagla, who served as foreign ministers at different intervals under P. M. Shastri and Mrs. Gandhi, have stated that they sought the advice of the senior officers in the External Affairs Ministry on a regular basis. See: J. Bandyopadhyaya, *The Making of India's Foreign Policy* (New Delhi: Allied Publishers, 1970), p. 170.

5

India's Political Process: Its Influence on Foreign Policy

A wide variety of forces from outside the government pressure the policymakers and influence their decisions both in the domestic and foreign realms. Political parties, economic and social interest groups, and the communications media all participate in the political process with the aim of influencing public policy. The more fully developed a democratic political system, the more vigorous is the activity of these nongovernmental agencies. The degree of success a group of people outside the government achieves in swaying the decisions of policymakers depends largely on its numerical strength, its economic base, and its access to the ruling group. While nongovernmental groups exercise near negligible influence on India's foreign policy, their presence and participation in the political process warrants consideration of their activities and influence.

Indian Political Parties and Foreign Policy

It is not uncommon to come across the statement in books written about the Indian political system that India has in effect a one party system. This conclusion is based for the most part on one primary factor: In the first general elections held in India in 1952, the Indian National Congress succeeded in occupying nearly 75 percent of all seats in the lower house of Parliament. The party had similar success in the general elections of 1957, 1962, and 1971. The 1967 elections were an exception to this pattern. On this occasion the Congress won a very slim majority, securing 282 seats out of a possible 521. Also, in 1969 the Indian National Congress Party split from within. This led to the creation of the "New" Indian National Congress and the "Old" Indian National Congress.[1] While it is true that in the general elections of 1971, the Indian National Congress (N), led by Mrs. Indira Gandhi, achieved a resounding majority thus once again establishing the Congress domination, the label of one party system is not entirely representative of the Indian political scene.

One party dominance has prevailed in India since independence for multiple reasons. However, a large number of parties have participated, freely and actively, in the political process from the beginning, and members owing allegiance to nearly a dozen different parties have been elected to both houses of Parliament. All media of communication have been available to non-Congress parties to mobilize public support. On the other hand, certain key factors such as lack of financial resources, inefficient organization, intraparty politics and ideological conflict, and the association of names like Gandhi, Nehru and Patel with the Indian National Congress during the preindependence and postindependence period, have prevented the non-Congress parties from acquiring any significant strength at the center.

> It would . . . be wrong to conclude that the Congress has held a 'monopoly of power' in India. Even before 1967 this was not true. For one thing there has always been a multiplicity of political parties opposing the Congress and some of these have succeeded in dislodging the Congress from power (in state governments). In votes the combined strength of the non-Congress parties and candidates has always been more than that of the Congress. . . . Even in seats the Congress has never commanded an absolute majority in all the (state) assemblies. And except for two brief spells in 1952–53 and 1963–64 the Congress alone has not ruled the entire country.[2]

It would not be wrong to conclude, however, that the safe majorities enjoyed by the Indian National Congress in the Central Parliament have permitted the ruling group to wield a completely free hand in writing India's foreign policy. The opposition parties have expressed strong disagreement with the foreign policy orientation of the party in power, in Parliament as well as in campaign literature, but their effectiveness in restraining the policymakers or changing the content and conduct of Indian foreign policy has been very limited. The government has moved with the confidence that it can secure a consensual response from its party members on any issue. This does not mean that there is a general agreement on foreign policy decisions within the ruling party. The fact of the matter is that there is little discussion or debate on foreign policy issues within the party at large.

Indian National Congress—The Ruling Party— and Foreign Policy

In a way the broad guidelines of Indian foreign policy lie in the many resolutions that were passed by the Indian National Congress during the period of the struggle for freedom. (Whenever the Congress party is mentioned here the reference is to Indian National Congress (N), the party presently in power.) The handiwork of Nehru, these resolutions embodied his thinking and his analysis of world politics. When the Congress took over the reins of government, it was expected that the party would influence government decisions. But the relationship between party and government established by Nehru cut off the party from interfering with the day to day governmental operations.[3] In the area of foreign affairs this practice seemingly continues to prevail.

> ... during the Nehru era ... on account of the predominant role played by Nehru as the maker of foreign policy both for the Congress and for the government of India, the distinction between the role of the party and that of the government had been virtually obliterated. In the post-Nehru era, on the other hand, due to the almost complete lack of interest in foreign policy on the part of the 'party bosses,' the undivided Congress Party seemed to have voluntarily surrendered its right and responsibility with regard to the making of foreign policy to the government, with the result that the 'bosses' often made the *ex post facto* discovery that some of the policies of the government had not been consistent with what they considered to be the general approach of the party to international affairs.[4]

It should be noted, however, that the structure of the Congress Party and that of the Parliamentary Administration runs on parallel lines. The All India Congress Committee, which represents the total membership of the party and acts in its behalf, is considered parallel to the Parliament. Similarly, the Working Committee of the Congress Party, in effect the executive body of the party and often referred to as the "high command," is considered parallel to the Government Cabinet. Also, the important members of the Cabinet are always members of the Working Committee of the Party. But those who are involved in party organization have always felt that the organizational wing occupies a status inferior to the Parliamentary wing. This is somewhat borne out by the comparative power and status of the prime minister to the Congress president. In reality the prime minister has always picked the president of the party. This was true in the days of Nehru, and has been firmly confirmed by the actions of current prime minister, Indira Gandhi.[5] Also, in Nehru's view, the supremacy of the Parliamentary wing over the organizational wing was necessary for a smooth and effective relationship between the party and government.

Even though the system appears to be well established, some avenues have existed all along which on the one hand provide the appearance that the party is consulted by the government, and on the other hand permit the government to prepare the party members in advance so that the process of seeking support from the party for government policy is expedited.

The Foreign Department of the All India Congress Committee, the Standing Committee on External Affairs of the Congress Parliamentary Party, the Congress Parliamentary Party, and the Congress Parliamentary Party Executive, are the four agencies of the ruling party that are expected to provide the party input on foreign policymaking.

The Foreign Department of the All India Congress Committee owes its birth to a resolution passed at the annual session of the party in 1925. The Department was created with the sole purpose of looking after the interests of the Indians living abroad. However, the department lay dormant until 1936, when Nehru first became the president of the Indian National Congress Party. Under his guidance the department concentrated its efforts on publicizing abroad India's struggle for independence, and establishing contacts with sympathetic individuals and organizations who could exert pressure on their governments to speak on behalf of Indian independence.

Once India became a sovereign state, the major function of the Foreign Department of the party lost its meaning. However, the agency did not fade out; it assumed a new character and continues to function. Immediately after independence, the Foreign Department served as a handy instrument to maintain close contact with freedom movements in the French and Portuguese enclaves on Indian territory. That the French and Portuguese were compelled to relenquish their control over those possessions can be partially attributed to the Department's efforts. Also in the postindependence era, the Department has attempted to keep in touch with ruling parties in other countries of the world, and has encouraged the exchange of visits between party officials. There is another activity that draws this agency into the international arena: The Foreign Department is involved in supporting and encouraging anticolonial movements in Africa and other places. But the initiative taken in this regard is of a minor nature. That, too, is mostly a projection of the Government's policy in this field and, therefore, cannot be calculated to have any impact on foreign policymaking. "In general, organizational leaders of the Congress, especially the relatively conservative among them, have always tended to view foreign policy with supreme indifference, almost verging on contempt. In fact, there seems to have always been a direct connection in India . . . between political conservativism and lack of interest in foreign policy."[6]

In the same vein, commenting on a suggestion of the "Reorganization Committee," created to recommend organizational changes to bring about greater interaction between party and government, the Congress Working Committee said in 1960: "Foreign Affairs, in our opinion, is too delicate a subject to be handled by any committee of the A.I.C.C."[7]

The Parliamentary Standing Committee on External Affairs is an arm of the Congress Party in Parliament. On paper this agency is expected to provide a continual dialogue on foreign affairs between the executive and the legislative wings of the party in power. But the fifty or so members of parliament who are on this committee, selected simply by making their desire for membership known to the Party Whip, are not specialists in international politics. The committee meets rarely. Such occasions are used by the foreign minister or the senior officials of the External Affairs Ministry to brief the members on government policy regarding selected issues so that no embarrassing questions are raised by the party members in parliamentary discussion. Committee members are free to express opinions and to seek clarification in these meetings. There is, however, no possibility of amending a policy already decided upon and ready for implementation.

The parent body of this committee is the Congress Parliamentary Party. Composed of all the members of the Congress Party in Parliament, it assumes a certain significance in both domestic and foreign policymaking. The Parliamentary Party has a minimum of two meetings during each session of Parliament; in addition the prime minister may call emergency meetings. These meetings allow all party members to express their views on specific foreign policy issues. Theoretically, a very large segment of the membership expressing a strong feeling on any given foreign policy issue could influence the prime minister and foreign minister to the extent of causing a change in policy adopted or contemplated. However, this has never happened, nor is it likely that an impressive majority of the party membership would initiate such action. The prime minister and foreign minister have used these meetings as a forum to justify India's international posture and in turn receive the acceptance by party members. However, the potential capability of the body to make an input is there. In 1969 when the old guard of the

Congress Party attempted to oust Mrs. Gandhi from the Prime Ministership and Party, it was the overwhelming majority support of the Parliamentary Party that sustained her in power and enabled her to lead the wing that now rules the country.

The Executive Committee of the Congress Party in Parliament is by far the most influential of all the organs of the party in power. Inasmuch as the prime minister selects the most prominent of the party leaders to sit on the Committee, he or she takes serious note of the sentiments expressed by members of the committee on domestic or foreign policy. This is not to say that this Committee makes a major contribution to foreign policy formulation on a continuing basis; however, it does have the power to exert influence if it chooses to do so. An ex-foreign service official turned academician mentions in his book that after the debacle of the Sino-Indian war in 1962, it was pressure exerted by this committee which was responsible for the resignation of the then defense minister Krishna Menon. The author, however, cites another incident in which the Committee failed in its attempts to oust Dinesh Singh, foreign minister for a short period under Mrs. Gandhi. Therefore, he suggests: "Such evidence . . . proves the political powers of the Parliamentary Executive, and its ability to offer effective *ex post facto* criticism of aspects of foreign policy, rather than to exercise positive *ex ante* influence on the making of foreign policy."[8]

Nonruling Parties and Foreign Policy

Parties not in power have little or no influence on foreign policy formulation. In a democratic system there are two major avenues open to parties not in power to influence government decisions. They can use the forum of the Parliament to debate, discuss, harass, and at times compel the majority party to yield to their viewpoint. Or else they can take their policy disagreements to the public, and hope that the people, either through the power of the vote or through direct contact with their representatives in Parliament, will influence the course of policy. Both these avenues, while available, prove mostly ineffective in achieving the desired objective.

The part played by the opposition in Parliament is discussed elsewhere. As regards the use of the public platform, nonruling parties in India cannot afford the luxury of expending their meager resources to focus major attention on foreign policy matters. Given the character of the electorate—close to seventy percent illiterate—to stress foreign policy as an issue or to make an attempt to inform the public at large about these government activities becomes meaningless. Parties do take care to make elaborate statements on foreign policy matters in their election manifestoes. Resolutions on international affairs are always an essential part of the business of party conferences. And there is without fail a unanimous agreement on these resolutions. But outside of these expressions of opinion, parties like the Swatantra Party, Praja Socialist Party, Samyukta Socialist Party, Jan Sangh, and the Communist Party of India provide no input in foreign policymaking.[9]

There are occasions when the parties out of power take advantage of a hot issue close to the heart of the voters, especially in the urban areas, and exploit public sentiment through such means as mass demonstrations. The maximum results achieved are two-fold. The ruling group is compelled to take note of the issue and explain its position in public, and they find it embarrassing to deal with a sensitive international issue in the open.

One minority party that pays a great deal of attention to foreign affairs is the Communist Party of India.[10] It has a Foreign Section located at its Central Office whose main functions are maintaining close relationships with Communist Parties in foreign countries, and keeping track of the stands taken by the Central Committee of the Communist Party of the Soviet Union on various international issues. The Foreign Section, thus, provides the guidelines which are followed by the Communist Party of India when it takes a stand on any foreign political matter before the Government. The Foreign Section of the CPI is also the force behind many front organizations such as the All India Peace Council and the Indo-Soviet Cultural Society. But while these organizations do have propaganda and agitational potential, in the final analysis the influence of the CPI on foreign policymaking is as negligible as that of the other minor parties.

Pressure Groups and Foreign Policy

The emergence of associational groups with the specific purpose of influencing government policy is a common feature of the democratic political system. Pressure groups or interest groups, as these associations are called, vary on the basis of their interest orientation. Some associations emphasize economic interest, while others press their claim on cultural, ideological, and social matters. But the intensity of the operations and the success of the pressure groups depends largely on the state of the political and economic environment of a given society. Reflecting on the lack of effectiveness of pressure groups on the Indian scene, one author writes:

> ... let us repeat that it is governmentalization of social and economic structures that provides the dominant framework of articulation in India

... the role of the party system and governmental interest groups are institutional rather than associational ... there is in India a persistent tendency to accord a low salience of recognition and legitimacy to associational interest groups. Trade and business associations, farm lobbies, even trade unions are not considered legitimate bases for political bargaining. If they are to make themselves felt, they ought to operate in and through party and bureaucratic structures. Then there is the context of a mixed economy: As government is the principal legitimate instrument for change and modernization, there is no place for 'interest groups' except as they are mediated through agencies that have a claim to the government's attention, namely parties and factions.[11]

There are three main types of interest groups that have exhibited some interest in the foreign affairs of India: (1) Business associations with an interest in investments abroad as well as governmental export-import policies; (2) ethnic associations that have expressed concern over the welfare of native populations overseas, and the immigration policies of the government; and (3) cultural organizations interested in spreading a common ideology as a base for the foreign policy of a community of nations.

Business Community and Foreign Policy

The Federation of Indian Chambers of Commerce and Industry, the most active and formidable entity among organized business and commercial interests, has spoken on some scattered issues relating to international affairs. The oldest among business associations, organized some 40 years ago, the Federation expressed strong objection to the separation of Burma from India in 1936. Again when the Indo-Burma Immigration Agreement was signed in 1941, the FICCI, seeing a threat to the economic activities of Indians in Burma, joined other ethnic associations in expressing sharp protest over the agreement and in asking for its revision. However, once India became independent, a two-fold development prevented the Federation and other business associations from displaying too keen an interest in foreign affairs. The constant theme of "socialism" projected by the ruling party resulted in a partial intimidation of the business houses. These associations began to concentrate on demonstrating their friendly attitude toward their own government, while their focus of attention was drawn more toward domestic economic interests.

Speaking before an annual session of the FICCI, Prime Minister Nehru said: "... it is not necessary for you to ask me or my government to take interest in Indians in Burma or Indians overseas anywhere else. It is our duty. We intend, and we are trying, to do our utmost for them."[12]

Clearly, while the business associations expressed their views on certain international matters in the preindependence period, and continue to do so now, their net effect has remained inconsequential. Since foreign policy was dictated from Whitehall during the period of British control, no groups or associations in India had any effect on British India's foreign policy. On the other hand, the practices of independent India's government have also discouraged the associational groups from making any contribution to foreign policymaking.

It should also be noted that India has not yet reached the stage of industrialization or capital accumulation where business interests have or contemplate heavy investments abroad. Furthermore, with the dedication of the government to a "socialistic pattern of society," and given the general state of the national economy, the administration exercises strict control over all economic policy which, of course, includes the import-export activity and capital investment abroad. And while a different trend may emerge in the future, so far the business interest groups have made no impact on India's foreign policy.

Ethnic Groups and Foreign Policy

The course pursued and results achieved by "ethnic" and "cultural" associations in India reveal a pattern identical to that of business associations. It is true that India does not have ethnic minority groups like the Italian, Irish and Polish Americans of the U.S.A. But the presence of sizeable Indian minorities in countries like Ceylon, Burma, and parts of Africa has given rise to associations that have attempted to plead the case of these Indians overseas. These associations, however, are weak and they have no impact on India's posture towards the countries involved.

In the aftermath of the Chinese occupation of Tibet, between 1950 and 1959, large numbers of Tibetan refugees crossed into India and were granted asylum by the Indian government. Most of the refugees settled in the subdistrict of Kalimpong, located near the border between Tibet and India. Before long the refugees formed into distinct groups on the basis of their ethnic and regional background. Despite the strict security measures of the Chinese on the Tibetan borders, close contact continued to exist between Tibetans in Kalimpong and their relatives and friends inside Tibet. The refugees were successful in supplying the rebel elements inside Tibet with arms and ammunition as well as propaganda literature. In 1958 all the elements within Tibet in revolt against Chinese control united to form the national group "Chul-ka Sum." Tibetan exiles in

Kalimpong were encouraged to constitute a similar unit on Indian soil, and send all the help they could to Tibet. Some sixteen different groups in exile did unite and proceeded to smuggle men and material into Tibet in support of the rebellion. The Chinese government protested against these activities, yet the Indian Socialist Party and the Praja Socialist Party heartily supported the cause of the Tibetans. Prominent Socialist leader Jaya Prakash Narain organized demonstrations to pressure the Indian government into actively aiding the emigres in their attempts to free Tibet from Chinese domination. After the Tibetan ruler, the Dalai Lama, took refuge in India in March, 1959, J. P. Narain urged the prime minister to recognize the Dalai Lama as the head of the Tibetan government in exile. But Nehru resisted all these attempts, and the events had no influence on India's overall policy or her posture vis-à-vis China at this stage.

Indian Muslims constitute a group which should be expected to express great interest in foreign policy matters such as Indo-Pak relations, Indo-Arab relations, and Indo-Israeli relations. But the history of Pakistan's creation, and Hindu-Muslim relations in general, has created that awkward situation whereby India's Muslim population must rely heavily on the government for its security and welfare. The result is that associations like the All India Muslim Legislators' Convention have repeatedly expressed their approval of India's policy towards Pakistan and other Muslim countries. The pro-Arab and anti-Israel posture of India is, of course, quite acceptable to Indian Muslims. But were this to be reversed, Muslims would still find it very difficult to take a stand opposed to that of the administration. Having opted to stay in India after the creation of a separate state for Muslims, Pakistan, these Muslims cannot afford to have their first allegiance to India questioned on any count. Thus "... none of India's present minority groups can be accurately described as interest groups actively attempting to influence Indian foreign affairs. This generalization also holds true for the various regions of India. Vast, diverse and linguistically fragmented though India is, no regional outlooks regarding any aspects of Indian foreign policy can be said to have emerged to date, let alone organized private regional associations speaking out on that policy."[13]

Cultural Groups and Foreign Policy

There are several associations in India which claim to be "peace" oriented or "culture" oriented. Organizations like the All India Peace Council, All India Progressive Writers' Association, All India Association of Democratic Lawyers, and many Friendship and Cultural societies, have all issued statements on occasions and passed resolutions at their meetings dealing with aspects of Indian foreign policy. However, these groups are recognized on the Indian scene as being front organizations dominated by and large by the Communist Party of India. Thus while their fundamental character affords them little influence on India's foreign policy, their activities are numerous and their efforts to propagandize Indo-Soviet friendship are ceaseless.

When the one-time defense minister Krishna Menon, who was forced into political exile after India suffered a humiliating defeat at the hands of China in 1962, once again entered politics by winning a seat in the Indian parliament with the support of the Communist Party in June 1969, the All India Peace Council sponsored his visit to the Soviet Union "to study the life of the Soviet people." Similarly, exchange of visits by prominent men of letters and politicians from both sides has been arranged by the Indo-Soviet Cultural Society. The association also has an active program of providing scholarships for Indian students interested in studying in the Soviet Union.

For a few years in the 1960s the Communist front organizations did carry on a campaign to have the Indian government establish full diplomatic relations with North Viet Nam and the German Democratic Republic. India raised her trade mission in East Berlin to the Consulate level in August 1970; it has now been elevated to the Embassy level. India's Consulate in North Viet Nam was raised to Embassy level in January, 1972. However, facts fail to establish any direct link between the pressure tactics of the Communist front organizations and the actions of the Indian government. Trade relations with the German Democratic Republic began as early as 1956. India proceeded to upgrade the diplomatic contact only when it was clear that the Bonn regime wished to improve its own relations with East Germany and did not object to similar action on the part of other states. On the other hand, whatever other reasons there might have been for establishing full diplomatic relations with North Viet Nam in January, 1972, it is not farfetched to surmise that after India's Soviet-backed victory in Bangladesh, she was quite willing to make a gesture that would please the Soviet Union. Further, India's move was an irritant to the U.S.A. and China, who had backed Pakistan against India. But while Communist front organizations have displayed keen interest in select foreign policy issues, very much like other pressure groups, they exert negligible influence on India's foreign policymaking.

Public Opinion and Foreign Policy

Scholars and leaders alike emphasize the fact that a democratic government cannot ignore public opinion in making policy, be it domestic or foreign. But there still remain questions to which there are no easy answers. How do you measure public opinion? Is there one public or are there many publics? And if the latter be the case, to which public should the policymaker respond? And the thorniest of all questions—how informed is public opinion? In dealing with a subject like foreign affairs, one soon realizes that much information in this area remains secret, and that, furthermore, information fed to the public is managed at many levels.[14] Thus a great deal of misinformation is passed around, and the situation calls for the public to have the vigilance and the ability to sift through the information for meaningful opinion. Therefore, even in the most literate and dynamic democracies, the role of public opinion in influencing foreign policy is severely limited and remains questionable.

India presents a special case in this regard. For centuries, mostly due to foreign occupation, the political environment discouraged the average Indian from expressing an opinion on public affairs. Moreover, even today nearly seventy percent of the population can neither read nor write. These people are, therefore, beyond the reach of newspapers as well as other forms of literature. Audiovisual means of communication are being developed rapidly, but their coverage to date is nominal. Until June, 1972, only the capital city of New Delhi was covered by single channel television transmission. In April, 1972, a mere 44,055 persons owned television sets out of a population of nearly five hundred and fifty million. The number of radio sets licensed amounted to approximately 15 million.[15] It is apparent, therefore, that at the present time resources do not exist in India to generate mass "public opinion," nor is there the will to articulate on the part of the public at large. It must also be noted that both radio and television are under government control,[16] and whatever means are there are utilized mostly by the ruling group to mobilize support for government policy. This leaves little room for public opinion input in a sensitive area like foreign policy.

Public opinion is not a phenomenon totally absent from the Indian scene, nor do India's policymakers completely ignore this area. On matters of local concern, Indian masses have on several occasions demonstrated their ability to organize and exert pressure.[17] But in foreign affairs the public response made itself manifest only in periods of crisis and on select issues, and that too, in most cases, subsequent to the implementation of initial policy.

> The Government of India has been helped, in fact, to a great extent compelled, to stick to a firm attitude towards Pakistan, especially on the question of Kashmir, by domestic public opinion. . . . Growing public opinion in favor of strong action in Goa was claimed by both Nehru and Krishna Menon to be a determinant in the shift of official policy in 1961. The mass upsurge on the occasion of the Chinese aggression in 1962 was partly responsible for a reorientation of Nehru's China policy. Angry

public opinion resulting from India's abortive attempt to participate in the Islamic Conference at Rabat compelled Mrs. Gandhi and Dinesh Singh to offer apologetic explanations and to be subsequently cautious with regard to their West Asia policy.[18]

Also, the March, 1972, elections to the state assemblies reflected how public opinion surfaces to manifest approval or disapproval of certain policies. The elections took place soon after India's smashing victory in the fourteen day Indo-Pak war of December, 1971. Public approval of the government's policy prior to the war, during the war, and in the aftermath of the war, was indicated by the fact that Prime Minister Gandhi's wing of the Congress Party won clear majorities in all the state assemblies with the exception of two states and a union territory. And in twelve states her party won by a two-thirds majority.

Apparently, public opinion in India remains a factor which the policymakers can ill afford to ignore. However, public opinion responds mostly in periods of crisis, and then too it reacts after the implementation of policy rather than at the initial stages of policy formulation. Furthermore, no system of repeatedly measuring public opinion on foreign policy issues has thus far been developed in India. No private agency has attempted to enter this arena. Putting together the wherewithal necessary to conduct such an exercise on a regular basis would be an expensive proposition. With no profit or benefit present as a return private enterprise cannot be expected to take up the task. And the government itself has shown little interest in initiating efforts to ascertain the views of either the academicians or the journalists.

> As regards academicians, journalists and other professional elite groups interested in foreign policy, their influence on decision making presupposes both sufficient expertise on their part and the willingness on the part of the government to ascertain their opinion. In India, it seems, there is deficiency at both ends, although Mrs. Indira Gandhi is known to have consulted some journalists from time to time on matters of both domestic and foreign policy.[19]

Thus the role played by public opinion in foreign policy formulation remains complex and of an uncertain nature.

The Press and Foreign Policy

In December, 1962, the director of the International Press Institute, commenting on developments in the world's press during the year, said:

> In Asia, the Indian Press has notably maintained its great traditions, even to the embarrassment of an immensely popular prime minister,

himself a protector of Press Freedom. In the great national firment which has followed the Chinese invasion, there has been clear evidence that the Press of India is free, vigorous and active.[20]

Until 1975 when under the umbrella of an emergency Mrs. Gandhi imposed strict press censorship, India's press was ranked by many as the highest in importance in Asia in terms of size, free circulation, and influence. But certain characteristics of the Indian Press and the environment within which it operates make it quite clear that there is a great distance between the Indian press and the halls of decision-making. The press does not have a direct input into policymaking even in the most developed of democracies such as the United States.[21] But it performs functions which are the lifeline of a democratic political system. In the sensitive area of foreign affairs, there are primarily two ways in which the press can and does make its impact felt. Firstly, the press disseminates news about foreign affairs and about foreign countries. While the government in power has varied and exclusive sources of information in this area, for the public at large the newspapers remain the only independent source of information. This is especially true of India where both the radio and the television media are owned and supervised by the government and have very meager coverage. Secondly, through its comments in the editorial pages, and the views expressed in special columns written by knowledgeable sources, the press attempts to mold public opinion in an area too specialized for the average citizen. But again, the impact of the press is dependent upon the character of its readers, the character of its news coverage, and factors such as circulation and access to newsmakers and newsworthy events.

In 1971 the population in India stood at 547 million. Of these, 165 million were listed as literate. They were served by 702 daily newspapers, which have a total circulation of 7.8 million. Thus it is estimated that the diffusion rate of Indian newspapers is less than 15 per 1,000 population. UNESCO has suggested that for effective communication the minimum dissemination rate should be 100 copies per 1,000. The vast masses of India, some 70 percent of the total population, remain unexposed to the influence of the press.[22]

The press in India has to bear some unusual burdens. Unlike the Constitution of the United States, the Indian Constitution does not specifically guarantee the freedom of the press. While it does guarantee freedom of speech and expression, this was diluted by amendments in 1951 and 1963, permitting the government to impose "reasonable restrictions" on this right in the interest of "sovereignty and integrity of the country," and in the interest of friendly relations with foreign states or public order, decency or morality, or on the ground of contempt of court, defamation or incitement to an offense.

> Nothing published in Communist China, North Korea, North Viet Nam and Taiwan is at present allowed to come into India. The ban extends even to Mainland press reports and other Chinese material translated by the United States Consulate-General in Hong Kong.... Even books and journals published in other countries, which are considered by the government to be unsympathetic to India are banned.... Particular issues of the *China Quarterly*, a scholarly journal on China published in the United Kingdom, are often confiscated by the customs authorities.... The recent decision of the government to discontinue the circulation of monitored foreign radio broadcasts among Members of Parliament and eminent journalists is also a definitely retrograd step from the point of view of an informed public opinion on foreign policy.[23]

Access to the newsmakers and events is highly limited for the Indian press. "There is in India ... no undeniable right of access for the press. Nor is there any powerful move to demand it."[24] While proceedings of the Central Parliament are freely covered and reported, news of the rest of the world does not fare too well. There is a two-fold problem. The Press Trust of India, the India news agency owned by Indian papers, can only afford to station a few correspondents abroad. They are located in what are considered to be the most important centers of the international arena. For the rest of the coverage the Indian press depends largely on foreign news agencies such as Reuters, United Press of America, and Tass. To add to its woes the production costs for the Indian Press are extremely high.[25] Seventy-five percent of the newsprint is purchased abroad. Furthermore, the new newsprint policy of the government has placed a strict quota on the amount of newsprint allocated to newspapers.

On occasion, in its past, the Indian press has spoken with full force on certain international issues,[26] at times in opposition to the government's stand. But too many factors deter it from being an effective influence on foreign policy matters. When it comes to formulation of India's foreign policy, the press appears to play no role.

Notes

[1] The party currently in power is popularly referred to as Congress (N) or Congress (R), whereas the group thrown out of power continues to use the name Indian National Congress, but is referred to as Congress (O).

[2] Rajni Kothari, *Politics in India* (Boston: Little, Brown and Company, 1970) p. 171.

[3] See remarks by Krishna Menon in *India and World Politics*, pp. 252–53.

[4] Bandyopadhyaya, *The Making of India's Foreign Policy* (New Delhi: Allied Publishers, 1970), p. 115.

[5] Congress President Kamraj can be said to have handpicked the successors to both Prime Minister Nehru and Prime Minister Shastri. But in 1969, a power struggle between the Party president and the current prime minister resulted in reestablishing the old practice of dominance of the prime minister over the Party president.

[6] Bandyopadhyaya, *India's Foreign Policy*, p. 119.

[7] *Indian Affairs Record*, New Delhi, June 1960, p. 123.

[8] *Indian Affairs Record*, p. 121.

[9] Portions of the major national parties' manifestoes dealing with foreign policy are included in the Appendix.

[10] In 1964 there was a split in the Communist Party of India. The result was the emergence of two Communist parties, one Moscow-oriented and one Peking-oriented. Reference above is to the Moscow-oriented Communist Party which is known as the CPI.

[11] Kothari, *Politics in India*, p. 218.

[12] Quoted by Richard J. Kozicki in "Indian 'Interest Groups' and Indian Foreign Policy," *The Indian Journal of Political Science*. Vol. 19, 1958, p. 223.

[13] Ibid., p. 225.

[14] The *Pentagon Papers* and the *Anderson Papers* provide good examples of this.

[15] These figures were reported by *The Times of India*, April 12, 1972.

[16] At a meeting of the Consultative Committee of Parliament for the Ministry of Information and Broadcasting, Prime Minister Gandhi said that there was no proposal before the government to separate television from All India Radio, the agency in charge of all audio and visual media of communication. *The Times of India*, April 12, 1972. At the same meeting, Mrs. Gandhi said that the government would consider the question of election broadcasts by political parties. She said that in the absence of agreement among political parties in this regard, the Election Commission gave up the idea at the time of the 1971 elections.

[17] The issues of cow slaughter, national language, and "linguistic states" have generated a quick and heated response from the public, which the government was forced to consider in its final decisions.

[18] Bandyopadhyaya, *India's Foreign Policy*, p. 109.

[19] *Ibid*. A research unit by the name of Institute for Defense Studies and Analysis came into existence around 1965. The director of the Institute, as well as many members, belongs to the Indian Administrative Service. Many of them were in the Defense Ministry at one time, but left the agency because of little opportunity for research. While the Institute is government supported, and there is a trend toward encouragement of research and analysis in the field of defense and foreign policy, the input of this organization in foreign policymaking is negligible. However, the Institute does publish a journal and scholarly analysis of international events in its quarterly reports.

[20] Quoted in *Seminar*, New Delhi, February 1963, p. 13.

[21] See a discussion of this in *The Foreign Relations of the United States* by Michael Armacost, pp. 120–123.

[22] The figures were taken from *Seminar*, New Delhi, November 1971.

[23] Bandyopadhyaya, *India's Foreign Policy*, pp. 110–111.

[24] Chanchal Sarkar, *The Illustrated Weekly of India*. Bombay, May 15, 1966, p. 13.

[25] Indian newspapers are five times as expensive as British newspapers.

[26] In 1956 when the Egyptian crisis and the Hungarian crisis erupted almost simultaneously, the Indian press hailed the stand taken by the government on Egypt. However, when India opposed the four-power resolution on Hungary in the United Nations, and Prime Minister Nehru attempted to defend this position before the All India Congress Committee, the press severely criticized the government policy and the prime minister. Similarly, in the aftermath of the Chinese invasion in 1962, many attributed the departure of the then Defense Minister Krishna Menon from the Cabinet to the wave of protest led by the Indian press. Krishna Menon himself denied this. In his interviews with Michael Brecher, quoted elsewhere in this book, Menon stated that the press as a whole did not affect policy making even though at times it had a negative effect.

6
Some General Characteristics of India's Foreign Policy

Relatively speaking India is a newcomer to the game of international politics.* Since 1947, when she joined the family of nation states, her foreign policy has reflected her change from an ex-colony, underdeveloped economically and militarily, asserting its independent will on a world scene dominated and fashioned largely by her previous masters, to a country that has come to reckon with and adjust to the reality of international affairs. The phenomenon is not a unique one in the post-World War II period.

It appears that the foreign policy of any nation state submits to two primary forces. First, in its day to day operations it responds both to new situations and the continuation of international crises. Second, the foreign policy of a nation state is affected by how the leadership making the foreign policy reads the international scene in a given period of time. It is expected that a policy always takes into account the capabilities of one's own state in relation to those of

---

*What follows is not a diplomatic history of India since independence. The attempt is to focus attention on those areas that have been the major concern of India's foreign policy in the last three decades.

other countries. These are the characteristics that give rise to inconsistency in the foreign policy of any state. Also, because of changes in political leadership, nation's capability and world conditions, the foreign policy of any state passes through many stages of development.

The developmental aspects of Indian foreign policy have been explored in the introductory chapter. It is significant that although India's foreign policy toward specific nations and regions has changed drastically, certain general characteristics have remained the same since independence, enhanced by a certain level of maturity that was lacking in earlier periods.

Nonalignment: The Trademark of Indian Foreign Policy

When Nehru took over the reins of India's foreign affairs, he let it be known from the start that India would follow an independent course in international affairs and not align herself with any group of nations. As head of the Interim Government, in his first broadcast to the nation on September 7, 1946, he said: "We propose, as far as possible, to keep away from the power politics of groups, aligned against one another, which have led in the past to world wars and which may again lead to disasters on an even vaster scale."[1]

At a time when the world was in the grip of severe tensions resulting from competition between U.S.A. and USSR, India's posture of nonalignment made no sense either to the West or to the East, and before long came under attack from both sides. John Foster Dulles, then a member of the United States delegation to the United Nations, remarked in New York: "In India, Soviet Communism exercises a strong influence through the Interim Hindu Government."[2] Later as the secretary of state in 1956, in a remark to the reporters he characterized the stance of nonaligned nations as "obsolete, immoral and shortsighted."[3]

The reaction of the Soviet Union was no different. Although the USSR had all along supported the Indian national movement, for a few years after 1948 Soviet newspapers, publications, and Moscow Radio were heavily critical of the Indian government. Nehru was accused of linking the fate of India with imperialist warmonger nations and his foreign policy was repeatedly branded as being proimperialist.[4]

Undiscouraged, Nehru continued to harp on the theme of nonalignment, justifying it in every way he could. On one occasion he maintained that the roots of this approach lay in India's ancient philosophical attitudes on life. On another occasion he attributed this posture to the teaching of Mahatma Gandhi. And then again on several occasions in Parliament he explained to members that practical consideration of economic and strategic interests left India no choice except to pursue a course of noninvolvement in the rivalries of the great powers.

The debate on the origins and meaning of nonalignment continues. Whether as a posture nonalignment and neutrality are interrelated or contradictory and incompatible remains a subject for scholarly scrutiny. The question is still raised as to how Nehru, as the spokesman of nonalignment, could say:

> We are neither blind to reality nor do we propose to acquiesce in any challenge to man's freedom from whatever quarter it may come. Where freedom is menaced or justice threatened or where aggression takes place, we can not be and shall not be neutral.[5]

And then again say:

> ... a country, placed as India is today, has inevitably to depend on other countries for certain essential things. We are not industrialized enough to produce all that we need. We have to depend on other countries for most of the things our Army or our Air Force or our Navy requires and are, therefore, dependent.[6]

The fact is that during the 1950s nonalignment proved a force to be reckoned with by both the U.S.A. and USSR, as it found adherents in Tito's Yugoslavia, Nasser's Egypt, Nkrumah's Ghana, Sukarno's Indonesia, U Nu's Burma and several other states in the Afro-Asian bloc of nations. While the Soviet Union and the United States were highly critical and unsympathetic toward nonalignment between 1947 and 1956, Nehru could credit his policy as the source for acceptance of India's counsel in such situations as the Indonesian struggle for independence, the Korean crisis, the 1954 Geneva accord, and the Suez Canal conflict in 1956.

More than anything else, nonalignment gave form to that newly realized spirit of independence which Nehru wished to manifest in thought and action. As the prime minister put it:

> By aligning ourselves with any one power, you surrender your opinion, give up the policy you would normally pursue because somebody else wants you to pursue another policy.... If we did align ourselves we would only fall between two stools.[7]

It is of some significance that Nehru viewed the struggle between the Soviet bloc and the anticommunist nations very differently than did the partisans on both sides. Nehru paid little heed to the viewpoint that the cold war was a battle of ideologies. Even as early as 1945, he wrote that the Four Freedoms and the Atlantic Charter were fading. He felt that the struggle between the United

States and the Soviet Union was of a purely military nature, of force against force, with philosophy playing no part. "In England, America, and Russia we revert to the old games of power politics on a gigantic scale."[8] Speaking before the Parliament in December, 1950, he said:

> The most relevant fact at the moment is that there are some great nations in this world with concentrated power in their hands that influence all the other nations. That being so, there is a conflict between these powerful nations. . . . Either these nations will have a war and try to suppress or defeat one another or one group will triumph over the other. There seems to be no other way. Although there is a great deal of talk about ideologies, I doubt if they come into the picture at all except as weapons.[9]

Interpreting the struggle between the Communist and the anti-Communist group of nations as mostly a phenomenon of power politics, India did not feel called upon to join a crusade for preserving democracy in the world: In her eyes that was not the issue at stake. The Indian leaders saw the cold war as primarily stemming from causes confined to the European theater, the product of past rivalries between the nations of Europe. Therefore, it was considered best for an Asian state like India to avoid entanglement in this conflict.

Moreover, in this power struggle between the mighty nations, Nehru did not see India threatened with aggression from either side. In a television interview in London in June, 1953, when asked if he saw any danger to India from Communist expansionist tendencies, he replied: "Well, whatever the internal position might or might not be, I see absolutely no danger—external danger—to India from Communist or any other source."[10]

Why was Indian leadership so certain that the Soviets would not endeavor to expand in the Asian direction by overt means? Firstly, it became clear by 1948 that Russia was relying heavily on native Communist parties to accomplish the desired goals by internal upheaval and subversion. Secondly, as Mao's Communists logged successive military victories against the forces of Chiang Kai-shek on the Chinese mainland, Asia was possibly considered as more appropriately the field of action for China. Thirdly, since India interpreted Russia's advance in the European theater as being a result of past European rivalries, any action connoting defense against a Russian military threat could have only raised the level of suspicion and tension between Russia and India. This would have been contrary to Indian interests for she was at this time attempting to secure Soviet support on such issues as Kashmir, Goa, and anti-colonial causes in the United Nations. And as onetime defense minister Krishna Menon put it, India did not react to the Russian expansionist tendencies "... because the Russians had not so far attempted to impose their will on India, while others had."[11]

India could not make common cause with the Soviet Union and the Chinese People's Republic due to India's democratic leanings and her economic dependence on the West. On the other hand, she could not afford the risk of increasing tensions with China and Russia by allying with the West, especially when India and China have a common border of over 2,000 miles. Looking at the international scene from this perspective, one can see that Nehru felt assured that nonalignment, *meaning nonparticipation in a military alliance*, was the most suitable posture for India during the 1950s.

India's economic needs in the postindependence period merit some attention in dealing with the nonalignment approach. Could India have solved her massive economic problems more easily by aligning herself with the Western nations, thus enabling her to draw more freely upon the vast resources of the United States?

India's economic problem is a chronic one. It was apparent at the time of independence that significant, top priority changes in the agricultural and industrial sectors were necessary to rapidly improve the situation. Alliances, said Nehru, stressed military preparedness more than anything else. In terms of India's interests, there was no problem that called for greater attention than the economic problem; cold war interests of the major powers emphasized ideological and military considerations. Speaking before the United Nations General Assembly, India's then representative, Mrs. Vijay Laxami Pandit, expressed this sentiment rather forcefully when she said:

> It has now become almost a platitude to say that a clash of ideologies underlies the rift that is so noticeable in the world today. We, who come from the East, who are intimately familiar with the dire want, the poverty and suffering and starvation that prevail there, may be forgiven for thinking that ideology is less important than practice. We cannot eat an ideology, we cannot brandish an ideology, and feel that we are clothed and housed. Food, clothing, shelter, education, medical services—these are the things we need.... The conflict of ideology, or whatever it may be, that is plunging the world into gloom and tension, seems so sadly irrelevant to these great human problems.[12]

India's economic ties with the West were close and there seemed no danger that India would be cut off economically if she failed to join with the West in a defensive alliance. In fact, by remaining nonaligned she could stick to her economic priorities and even draw upon Soviet economic aid, if the prospects opened up.

Given this background it is not hard to understand why India chose nonalignment; but the policy soon came under attack as being difficult to reconcile with Nehru's desires to see India play a dominant role in world politics. How could a nation heavily dependent on outside sources for basic economic and military necessities, pleading noninvolvement in the quarrels of major powers, dare to preach and seek to direct "right conduct" on the international scene?

Nonalignment was a mixture of success and failure. India took the initiative, or was encouraged by other nations to mediate on several occasions in the resolution of serious international crises. As early as 1947 India was in the forefront of a move in the UN Security Council to bring about Dutch departure from Indonesia. India was actively involved in the Indonesian problem until its resolution in December, 1949, when complete sovereignty was transferred to the Republic of the United States of Indonesia. India made every effort to assist in bringing the Korean war to a quick halt after its outbreak in 1950, and she played a key role in its final conclusion in 1953. India was not formally a participant in the Geneva Conference of 1954, which dealt with the Indo-China issue. But her emissary, Krishna Menon, was present at the Conference and made a significant contribution. When the Suez crises broke out in 1956, India acted with speed within the United Nations and outside it to find a settlement to the issue. During the decade after independence India's stature and influence in world affairs were such that suggestions were made that she be given a permanent seat in the U.N. Security Council.

Ironically though, while India was realizing a measure of success far from her own boundaries, nearer at home her foreign policy produced no positive results. India's territorial dispute with Pakistan over Kashmir remained unresolved, and was a constant source of friction and tension. India failed to persuade Portugal to hand over Goa, an enclave on Indian territory, which was a painful reminder of colonial days. Also, nonalignment did not deter the United States from signing a military aid pact with Pakistan in 1954, which heightened Indo-Pak tensions and further reduced chances of a negotiated settlement of the Kashmir issue. China's attack on India in 1962 over the boundary dispute on the northern borders in the Himalayas not only punctured the claims of a successful foreign policy, but also demonstrated that nonalignment was neither a substitute nor a source for military and economic strength.

For all practical purposes India's nonalignment posture was meaningless after 1962. Heightened security consciousness and fear of another possible attack by China softened India's resistance to security pacts. Finally, in 1971 when she feared that China would once again confront her, this time in partnership with Pakistan, India rushed to sign a defense pact with the Soviet Union.

Mrs. Gandhi attended the Algiers Conference of nonaligned nations in September, 1973, but the character of the 76 countries gathered together was testimony in itself that nonalignment as a policy or posture was now irrelevant. Mrs. Gandhi's attendance at the meeting did not escape notice, despite the presence of such leaders as Castro of Cuba, Emperor Haile Selassie of Ethiopia, President Sadaat of Egypt, Idi Amin of Uganda, King Faisal of Saudi Arabia, and Col. Khadafi of Libya. But the real value of this conference for India was embodied in the statement of the prime minister:

> The tendency is to expect instant results from such conferences. We have not come here to negotiate or to settle disputes. The outcome is bound to be intangible but no less substantial: to take back with us greater understanding and sense of comradeship, to return to our countries with renewed strength to work for our common ideals.[13]

While Prime Minister Gandhi insists that nonalignment continues as a guide for India's foreign policy, a posture of nonalignment holds little or no significance in a period when cold war politics has been replaced by détente. Moreover, since the United States considers it necessary to preserve her newly formed friendship with China to freeze the "world order" as it exists, India must continue to rely on the Indo-Soviet treaty as a measure of security against powerful China. This too makes a mockery of nonalignment. But India's policymakers have long justified their actions before the Indian public in the name of nonalignment. Therefore, this will remain New Delhi's trademark for many years to come.

Asia and Indian Foreign Policy

Independent India's leadership pursued a dual course of action toward the other nations of Asia. First, she tried to bind them into a united front which could pressure the major powers to leave Asia to the Asians. Second, India sought to carve for herself a role of leadership in the affairs of Asia. It has been noted earlier that the incentive for these goals came from the philosophical and psychological orientation of men like Tagore, Gandhi, and Nehru. India achieved partial success in both these goals, but as the realities of military and economic interest and the struggle for power among the contending elites pressed upon each state of Asia, each reached for her individual objectives independent of any integrated approach. India reluctantly but surely changed her pattern of dealing with these states. Accounts of India's anticolonial successes in the U.N., her fight for Indonesian freedom, and her role in Korea and the Geneva Conference in 1954 have been recorded earlier in this narrative. What needs to be emphasized here is the character and essence of change which marked India's Asian policy in the 1960s.

The Bandung Conference was possibly the last occasion to highlight India's influence in Asia. The original idea for this Asian-African Conference was supplied by the Indonesian prime minister at the time of the Colombo Conference, Ali Sastroamidjojo. The Bandung Conference, sponsored by the "Colombo Powers" opened at Bandung, Indonesia on April 18, 1955, with 29 Afro-Asian nations attending. Its significant feature was that it was history's first intercontinental conference of the non-European peoples.[14]

The Bandung Conference was at best an attempt to bring together countries united by a common detestation of colonialism and racialism, and a desire for a higher standard of living. The final communique of the conference revealed that those were the only subjects on which there was unanimous opinion. For the nations gathered together on this occasion represented not only a wide variety of cultures, but every conceivable political doctrine and economic system. Present in the assembly were countries like communist China, democratic India, Burma and Ceylon, the Islamic Republic of Pakistan, and monarchist Iran, Iraq, and Saudi Arabia. Then again some of these states were fully committed to one side or the other in cold war politics, while many stuck to nonalignment. No wonder that except for expressions of hope for future cooperation among Afro-Asian states, the conference accomplished little of substance.

Where India was concerned the Bandung Conference was not one of those occasions during which she was able to exercise powerful influence. If India was conscious of her important status in Asia, the presence of People's Republic of China prevented her from such an assertion. On the other hand Prime Minister Chou En-lai utilized the occasion to propagate the peaceful intentions of the new mainland China regime.

The Bandung Conference has been characterized by many as the high mark of Indian influence in the Third World. What is interesting is that 1954 was the year during which the United States signed a military pact with Pakistan over India's strenuous objections. The U.S. also drew Pakistan, Thailand, and the Philippines into the Southeast Asia defense treaty during 1954. As part of India's treaty of friendship with mainland China she was compelled to give up all territorial claims in Tibet. Thus in 1954 certain trends began eroding India's influence. America entered West Asia, South Asia and Southeast Asia to contain Communist expansion. India started leaning toward a closer relationship with China and the Soviet Union as their leaders exchanged visits during 1954 and 1955.

The fact is Geneva and Bandung had provided Mao's regime with its first opportunity to appear before the international community of nations after coming to power on mainland China in 1949.

India had played the leadership role in Asia with little challenge before 1954; Bandung was not only the first occasion when she had to share this role, but more significant still, in subsequent years as China's presence on the Asian and the global scene became ominous, India's role and influence in Asia and elsewhere faded. Ironically, it was the will and power of China, an Asian neighbor India had courted for more than a decade, that struck the blow in 1962 that brought India's influence to an all time low.

India has now abandoned all pretensions of leadership in Asia. She has come to recognize that in the face of China's rise as a formidable military power, and Japan's awesome economic buildup, her influence carries little weight in the capitals of Asia. In an interview in March, 1973, with Japan's daily *Asahi Shimbum*, Mrs. Gandhi spoke of her admiration for the energy and discipline of the Japanese people. She expressed the hope that "Japan will not be satisfied just by being only an Asian member of a rich man's club," but would play a role in international affairs commensurate with its economic strength and importance. She added that she wished to see Japan contribute to the stability in Asia and to the economic buildup of the countries in that part of the world.[15]

Gradually, India has begun to stress a bilateral approach, as opposed to her earlier collective approach, with other Asian nations. Her relations with Ceylon, now officially known as Sri Lanka, are comparatively smooth today. The problem of Indian minorities in Ceylon, which was a constant irritant, has finally been worked out to permit normalization of relations. Furthermore, by responding to Prime Minister Sirimavo Bandaranaike's call for help in putting down the revolt by suspected Maoist insurgents in April, 1971, India has earned the gratitude and prolonged friendship of the regime in power.

Relations with Burma are judged as "cool and cordial" by official circles in India. The two countries have succeeded in establishing a mutually acceptable modus vivendi. India's problem with the Naga rebels and Burma's problem with the Karen rebels in the areas adjoining the two countries has influenced the regimes in power to appreciate each other's difficulties and respect mutual territorial integrity and independence. Inasmuch as India, Burma, and China have common borders, ever since the 1962 conflict with China, India has been careful not to permit any developments which would result in the deterioration of her relations with Burma. The government of India turned down the request of former Burmese Prime Minister U Nu for political asylum in June, 1973, because New Delhi did not wish to antagonize the military regime of General Ne Win.

When General Ne Win released U Nu from jail in 1970, India allowed the deposed prime minister to undertake a pilgrimage to Buddhist shrines in India with the consent of the Burmese government. Soon after that U Nu decided to settle in Thailand. He is credited with having set up a command organization there to plan the overthrow of General Ne Win. Burma's protests to Thailand against U Nu's activities are not only causing embarrassment to the Thai government, but they have led to U Nu's request for shelter in India. Interestingly, India had no hesitation in giving refuge to Dalai Lama in 1959 over the strong protest of China. But in 1973, the pragmatic approach obviously prevailed, and U Nu has been denied the privilege of living in India.

In the past, India has failed to cultivate relations with the nations of Southeast Asia beyond the borders of Burma, but Prime Minister Gandhi has started a new trend by encouraging the exchange of state visits with these countries. High officials from India —the president, the foreign minister, and the prime minister herself —have visited Malaysia, Singapore, and Thailand, and dignitaries from these states have paid return visits to New Delhi. In addition, India has taken economic initiatives in Malaysia and Thailand. As a whole, however, the area is still far from settled despite official cessation of hostilities in Viet Nam. In answer to a question in Parliament regarding the possibility of India being involved in a security pact with the countries of Southeast Asia, India's external affairs minister Swaran Singh replied that the idea had to originate as a result of mutual contacts. He further commented that India "was not interested in concluding any military pact with countries in Southeast Asia but she would welcome any arrangement with these countries which would strengthen their security, safeguard their independence and bring about economic cooperation."[16] Thus India's future activities in Southeast Asia have yet to unfold.

Of course, India was greatly relieved to see the removal of the massive American arms buildup in Viet Nam. India's support of Hanoi's cause was consistently vigorous. India established full diplomatic relations with North Viet Nam in January, 1972, ignoring the adverse repurcussions in Saigon.

These are but the beginnings of India's new approach. The United States continues her presence in Southeast Asia; Sino-Soviet rivalry has by no means come to an end with the departure of U.S. troops from Viet Nam. The superpowers are engaged in fierce competition to police the Indian Ocean. These are factors that make for a complex and highly fluid situation in this part of the world. What new adjustments and accomodations India's foreign policy will be compelled to make in the future is a matter of great speculation.

Goa in Indian Foreign Policy

The day Britain transferred power to Indian hands, there still remained pockets of Indian territory under French and Portuguese control. About three centuries earlier when the European powers appeared on the South and West coast of India, they occupied some territories as their trading posts. When the British eliminated the rival European nations from the Indian trade and finally gained complete political control of India by the middle of the nineteenth century, they still left these trading posts in the hands of those powers who had originally occupied them. While India was herself under alien rule, she had no voice in regard to the existence of these foreign posts. However, the leaders of India had hoped that once Britain left, other nations holding small portions of her territory would follow suit and transfer these posts to India by peaceful negotiation. The towns of Pondicherry, Chandernagar, Karaikal, Yanam, and Mahe were under French rule while Goa, Diu, and Daman were under Portuguese control.

France and Portugal gave no indication that they were contemplating the return of their possessions to the government of India at the time of independence. There were widespread disturbances in French India and Portuguese India, with both Goans and Indians calling for integration. Nehru approached both France and Portugal for a negotiated settlement. After prolonged talks France agreed to hold a plebiscite in her colonies, and as a result ceded all her possessions to India by 1954.

Portugal pursued a different course. The Portuguese minister of colonies declared on June 10, 1947, that Portugal would fight to the last soldier to keep control of Goa and other possessions even after the British left India.

The Portuguese government refused to discuss the future of Goa when the Indian minister at Lisbon presented an aide memoire in February, 1950, seeking to begin talks on the issue. Defeated in these efforts India turned to the major world powers to support her cause and exert pressure on Portugal to settle the issue by mutual agreement.

Speaking on the occasion of India's seventh anniversary of independence, Nehru said:

> Goa has become a test for all nations. . . . Goa is the oldest symbol of (the) colonial idea in India. It is an ugly pimple and if anybody says that we should continue to tolerate this pimple, then he has not understood our mind and heart nor of Asia. . . .
>
> We have now to watch and see towards which side the nations of the world lean in the matter of Goa and what advice is given, then the

problem of Goa will be solved peacefully. If wrong advice is given, then tension and conflict is bound to increase.[17]

As it turned out, Nehru was to discover once again that cold war politics had global implications, and no nation—aligned or nonaligned—was exempt from its influence. In December, 1955, on the occasion of the official visit of Portuguese Foreign Minister Paulo Cunha to the United States, the then Secretary of State John Foster Dulles, in a joint communique, referred to the Portuguese provinces in the Far East and hinted that NATO shared the responsibility for the overseas possessions of Portugal. At a press conference on December 6, 1955, in answer to a reporter's question, Dulles said: "As far as I know, all the world regards it [Goa] as a Portuguese province. It has been Portuguese for about 400 years."[18]

For Nehru this was one more signal that the Western powers had chosen to support anti-Indian forces, as pressure or punishment for India's proclaimed nonalignment posture. Thus, notwithstanding contradiction or inconsistency, India found great satisfaction in Soviet Communist Party Chief Nikita S. Khrushchev's statement which amounted to a rebuttal to the Dulles statement. Speaking at a function organized by the Hindi Association in New Delhi on December 13, the Soviet leader said:

> ... The Portuguese conquered the territory 400 years ago. They enslaved it by force, violence and fraud. The fact that they did this 400 years ago does not invest the Portuguese with the right to maintain their domination any longer. Goa does not belong to Portugal and will have to go to the people to whom it belongs.[19]

However, the problem of Goa continued to simmer. On December 17, 1961, the Indian army marched on Goa. After a military campaign lasting barely 24 hours, India invaded and occupied the territory.

The Portuguese delegate to the United Nations requested an immediate meeting of the Security Council on December 18, 1961. The United States, Great Britain, France, and Turkey presented a resolution calling for immediate cessation of hostilities and withdrawal of Indian forces to positions held before December 17. As expected the Soviet Union vetoed this resolution.

The Goa problem thus ceased to exist as a major issue of Indian foreign policy after 1962. However, in the interval between 1947 and 1962, it affected Nehru's foreign policy in a major way. It confirmed Nehru's suspicions that there was little common ground between Indian interests and the interests of the major Western states. Further, even if India did not relish much closeness with the Soviet Union, it became clear that Russia was the power India could rely on for support when needed. Above all in the process of resolving the Goan issue Nehru had to reconcile himself to the fact, as painful as it might have been, that no state could renounce military means as an instrument of foreign policy.

In view of the eventual outcome, it seems unfortunate in India's view that the Western powers permitted the Goan problem to assume such major proportions within Indian foreign policy. But apparently policymakers shift with the prevailing winds on the international scene. On December 31, 1974, India and the new regime in Portugal signed a treaty restoring diplomatic relations which were severed in 1955. Under this treaty Portugal recognizes India's sovereignty over Goa, Diu, and Daman.

Kashmir in Indian Foreign Policy

Control of Kashmir became an international issue when the problem was put on the U.N. Security Council agenda at the initiative of India: Prime Minister Nehru wished to demonstrate his belief that lasting peace in the post-World War II period could be achieved only if all disputes among nation states were submitted to the United Nations for resolution.

British control over India had two facets. British India was directly administered by the central authority. There were some 562 "princely states" on the subcontinent which were administered internally by the native princes, but they were completely under British authority in matters of defense, foreign affairs and communications. At the time of transfer of power, Britain proclaimed that the princely states were free to decide their own fate, but recommended that they agree to join either the Indian Union or Pakistan. Most of the states followed this advice, but in three instances the otherwise smooth operation encountered trouble. Junagarh, Hyderabad, and Kashmir stood aloof and did not follow the example of the others who had all by August 15, 1947, accepted the Instrument of Accession and had surrendered to the Dominion of India or Pakistan control over defense, external affairs, and communications. However, Junagarh and Hyderabad soon also fell into the fold. But an ugly situation developed in Kashmir which even today continues to harass the governments of India and Pakistan.

Situated in northwest India, Kashmir covers an area of about 84,000 square miles. One of the largest princely states at the time of partition, it is uniquely situated. The boundaries of Kashmir touch the borders of China, Russia, and Afghanistan, and at the same time it is contiguous to both India and Pakistan. But at the time of Indian independence it was not strategic advantage sought either by India or Pakistan that created the issue. The religious friction and rivalry responsible for India's partition also sparked the conflict over ultimate control of Kashmir.

The population of Kashmir is 77 percent Muslim, while Hindus, Sikhs, and Buddhists account for the rest. In 1947 the state was ruled by a Hindu Maharaja. Up to the time of transfer of power, the Maharaja did not accede to either of the Dominions and toyed with the idea of continuing as an independent state. However, shortly before the transfer of power in August, 1947, the Kashmir government announced that it wanted to enter into a Standstill Agreement with India and Pakistan. Pakistan signed an agreement while India maintained that such a proposition had to be examined carefully before acceptance.

Not long after, the Maharaja of Kashmir complained that Pakistani authorities were coercing the state into acceding to Pakistan. On the evening of October 24, the Government of India received the news that about five thousand tribesmen had succeeded in capturing many towns and were only about 35 miles from Srinagar, the capital of Kashmir. The Maharaja of Kashmir sent desperate appeals for armed help to India. On the advice of the then Governor General Lord Mountbatten, India did not respond immediately. But when the Maharaja of Kashmir formally acceded his state to India, and the popular political party of Kashmir, All-Jammu and Kashmir National Conference concurred in the decision, Indian troops were quickly dispatched.[20]

Understandably, this act of accession by which Kashmir became a part of India was totally unacceptable to Pakistan. But India held on to the position that her actions were legal, and that furthermore popular leadership of Kashmir as represented by Sheikh Abdullah was behind her. If the circumstances under which the Maharaja of Kashmir had acted were far from normal, India felt that the blame lay at the door of Pakistan who had not only created the circumstances but in doing so had acted contrary to the spirit and words of the Standstill Agreement.

Fighting between Indian troops and tribes supported by Pakistani troops continued. While India succeeded in pushing back the invaders, parts of Kashmir remained in the hands of Pakistan. On December 22, 1947, in a communication to Liaquat Ali Khan, prime minister of Pakistan, India formally requested that his Government call upon the Pakistani nationals to stop participating in the attack on Kashmir and also deny the invaders all access to and use of Pakistani territory for operations against Kashmir.

Receiving no reply, India's representative at the United Nations placed the Kashmir problem before the Security Council on December 31. On April 28, 1948, the Security Council called for a plebiscite in Kashmir. But no agreement could be reached as to mutually acceptable conditions under which the plebiscite could be held, so the problem was unresolved. It is significant to note that once the Kashmir problem had reached the United Nations, it not only became important for India to win the support of other nations, it also became important to her that whatever defensive measures Pakistan took had to be met with countermeasures. It is no exaggeration to state that from 1948 onward, India's foreign relations have been influenced heavily by concern over the Kashmir issue.

Until 1962 the size and character of India's armed strength were dictated by the threat of Pakistan's occupation of Kashmir. In the Middle East, India elected to side with the Arab countries against Israel because India did not wish to see an alliance of Muslim nations supporting Pakistan. India's conduct in the United Nations after 1948 was patterned with one eye on Kashmir— mainly to make certain that the U.N. was blocked from passing any resolution that was antagonistic to India's interests in Kashmir. It became evident to India early in the Security Council debates that it was the Soviet Union that she had to court to save her from embarrassing and hostile U.N. resolutions, especially since the Western powers refused to accept at face value her charges against Pakistan. India became fearful when cold war considerations led the United States to seek out Pakistan as an ally in the antiexpansionist policy against the Soviet Union. The U.S.-Pakistan military aid pact of 1954 alienated India against the United States while it spurred the Soviet Union and India to further their contacts and friendship. As a pro-Soviet gesture India failed to join other nations in condemning Soviet aggression in Hungary and Czechoslovakia in 1956. In return India was saved on several occasions by the Soviet veto which blocked the Security Council from taking any action in Kashmir contrary to Indian interests. Thus India and the Soviet Union found common ground and reasons to coalesce on many issues within the United Nations and outside it.

The Kashmir issue triggered another armed clash between India and Pakistan in September, 1965. Pressure from major powers, in particular the USA, U.S.S.R., and Britain, upon whom both India and Pakistan relied heavily for military assistance, brought the war to a speedy end. Both sides accepted mediation by the Soviet Union, and in January, 1966, they concluded the Tashkent Agreement. The Agreement changed no boundaries; it did not create any machinery to deal with the real issues; it only secured for both sides a temporary period of détente.

The Kashmir issue remains unresolved. Indian and Pakistani troops continue to face each other across the cease-fire line which was accepted by the antagonists under the Security Council resolution of January, 1949. However, the events of December, 1971, which resulted in the severence of the eastern wing of Pakistan and the formation of the independent state of Bangladesh, have altered the situation radically. India now stands at a distinct strategic advantage in any future settlement of the issue. But until the problem is finally settled Kashmir will remain a focal point of Indian foreign policy and an irritant in Indo-Pak relations. It will also continue to be a source of regional instability on the subcontinent of South Asia.

Notes

[1] Jawaharlal Nehru, *India's Foreign Policy* (New Delhi: The Publications Division, Ministry of Information and Broadcasting Government of India, 1961) p. 2.
[2] *The Hindu* (Madras), January 21, 1947.
[3] *New York Times*, June 10, 1956.
[4] See M. Alexi Dykov in *New Times*, January 14, 1948, and January 12, 1959. See also A. Leoindov in *New Times*, August 4, 1948.
[5] *Jawaharlal Nehru's Speeches 1949–1953* (New Delhi: Publications Division Ministry of Information and Broadcasting Government of India, 1954), p. 125.
[6] *Ibid.*, p. 217.
[7] *Nehru's Speeches*, pp. 193–93.
[8] Jawaharlal Nehru, *The Discovery of India* (Calcutta: The Signet Press, 1946), pp. 655–56.
[9] *Nehru's Speeches*, p. 184. (Nehru observed in the Indian Parliament once: "How many countries of the free world have democracy?")
[10] *Amrit Bazar Patrika* (Calcutta), June 27, 1953.
[11] *The Statesman* (Calcutta), August 9, 1956.
[12] *Plenary Meetings of the General Assembly*, Vol. 1 (September 16–November 13, 1937), p. 137.
[13] *India News*, Embassy of India, Washington, D.C., September 14, 1973.
[14] *Asian-African Conference*, issued by the Information Service, Indonesian Embassy, New Delhi, n.d.
[15] *India News*, Embassy of India, Washington, D.C., March 16, 1973.
[16] *The Statesman Weekly* (Calcutta), June 3, 1972. It is significant to note that India is reluctant to take any initiative in Southeast Asia which might be misinterpreted and resented by China. Peking might also suspect that the action was instigated by the Soviets.
[17] *The Hindu* (Madras), August 16, 1954.
[18] *New York Times*, December 7, 1955.
[19] *The Hindustan Times* (New Delhi), December 14, 1955.
[20] Alan Campbell-Johnson, *Mission with Mountbatten* (London: Robert Hale, Ltd., 1951), pp. 223–226.

7

India and Her Neighbors

India and Pakistan

Situated along her western border, Pakistan as one of India's closest neighbors[1] is also her constant concern. Reasons for prolonged friction between these two countries range from the religious and ethnic to the economic and psychological. They go back deep into the history of the subcontinent. The British, anxious to transfer power to the peoples of the subcontinent after World War II, were persuaded to believe that partitioning the subcontinent into two separate states of "Hindu India" and "Muslim Pakistan" would resolve many issues and eventually result in stability in the area.[2] This put an end to the British dilemma, but for the peoples of these two states partition created new sources of suspicion, rivalry, and enmity.

Each of India's three prime ministers was involved in a war with Pakistan. Each sought to normalize relations in the aftermath of war. They were all encouraged by initial attempts. Total success alluded Nehru and Shastri. Whether Mrs. Gandhi's experience will be different, only time will tell.

Prime Minister Nehru went to war with Pakistan over Kashmir in 1948. It ended, without resolution, in a U.N. imposed cease-fire in 1949. After the cease-fire, under U.N. aegis, several attempts were made to settle the dispute. When all these efforts failed, India and Pakistan agreed that they should attempt to handle the matter through bilateral negotiations. In 1953, a number of meetings took place between Nehru and the then prime minister of Pakistan, Mohammed Ali. Before anything of substance could come out of these meetings, news surfaced that the United States and Pakistan were about to sign a military pact, which was executed in 1954. Inasmuch as Nehru considered this a slap at his nonalignment posture, and an attempt on the part of Pakistan to deal with India from a position of strength, the course of Indo-Pak negotiations faltered. The Kashmir issue was put aside and relations between India and Pakistan began a gradual decline.

In 1960 there appeared another opportunity to mend fences. In that year, with the mediation of the International Bank for Reconstruction and Development, India and Pakistan reached an agreement on the use of the waters of the Indus River System. At the time of the signing of the Indus Waters Treaty in September, 1960, in Karachi, both Prime Minister Nehru and the then president of Pakistan, Mohammed Ayub Khan, expressed the hope that it would lead to eventual settlement of all outstanding issues between the two countries. But this hope was never realized by Nehru in his lifetime.

Lal Bahadur Shastri, who took over as prime minister after Nehru in 1964, let it be known that nonalignment still remained the overall umbrella for Indian foreign policy. But under his nonalignment policy India did not preach to the superpowers or small powers. Shastri immediately set about to put India's relations with her neighbors on a more solid footing. Circumstances did not permit him to make much progress: In September, 1965, war broke out between India and Pakistan.

The confrontation began over a salt march in the disputed and undemarcated area of Rann of Kutch, located on the border between India and Pakistan on India's southwestern flank. In early April, 1965, Pakistani troops crossed into territory patrolled by Indian border police. This led to an armed clash and general mobilization was ordered in both countries. During May and June there were several skirmishes, but Britain's intervention brought about a cease-fire and an agreement that the matter be referred to an international tribunal. The territory was divided between the antagonists.

However, despite the settlement on this front, reports of activity on the Kashmir border soon surfaced. In August the Indian government became aware that outside elements were disrupting life in the capital city of Srinagar. Soon thereafter it was learned that Pakistani troops had attacked all along the Kashmir cease-fire line. The Indian army responded with full force. But to stop Pakistan from making any advance on the Kashmir front, on September 3 Prime Minister Shastri ordered Indian troops to march into Pakistan crossing the international boundary in Punjab.

At the urging of the United States, Britain, and the Soviet Union, the U.N. Security Council passed a resolution on September 4 calling for an immediate cease-fire. The warring nations ignored this call. Ever since 1962 India had feared that a situation of this kind would give China the excuse to intervene on Pakistan's behalf. When on September 16 China issued an ultimatum to the Indian government that if it did not demolish certain structures on the Tibetan-Sikkim border and return some "lost sheep and yaks" by September 18, China would take action to correct the situation, India's fears were realized. However, first the Chinese extended the deadline from September 18 to September 22. And then they failed to carry out the threat when Britain and the U.S. made it clear that any intervention by China would result in countermeasures by the two powers.

The U.S., Britain and the USSR were nonetheless anxious to stop the fighting. The U.S. and Britain halted all military and economic aid to the countries at war. Adopting a neutral posture, the USSR called upon India and Pakistan "to display reason and desist from further military action and take measures towards an immediate end to the hostilities between them." On September 23 the two parties called a halt to the fighting. As the Indian prime minister later stated, it was the pressure from big powers, especially the United States upon whom India depended for basic economic aid, that compelled him to agree to a cease-fire. It is not difficult to understand that neither India nor Pakistan had the capability to carry on a prolonged campaign when the major sources of their military supplies had been cut off.

Subsequent to the cease-fire all efforts by the United Nations to untangle the situation failed. While the brief war ended in more of a draw than anything else, there still remained in Indian hands a sizeable territory belonging to Pakistan. Eventually it was Soviet Prime Minister Aleksei Kosygin who played the role of mediator.

Prime Minister Shastri, President Ayub Khan, and Premier Kosygin began their talks at Tashkent, Russia, on January 3, 1966. Using all the tact and pressure necessary, Kosygin succeeded in having the two antagonists agree to the Tashkent Declaration of January 10, 1966. In the main the Agreement called for the two sides to withdraw all their personnel not later than February 25, 1966, to the positions they held prior to August 5, 1965. The Agreement also provided for further meetings between the representatives of India and Pakistan to normalize relations between the two countries. This goal, of course, was never achieved. There were some provisions in the Agreement that were interpreted by Indian circles as concessions awarded to Pakistan under pressure from the Soviet Union. Prime Minister Shastri did not get the opportunity to defend the course of action he had taken. He died of heart failure in the early hours of January 11, 1966, at Tashkent.

Soon after coming to power, Prime Minister Gandhi saw that her immediate task was to preserve India's special relationship with the Soviet Union and prevent her from becoming a close ally of Pakistan. The Tashkent Conference had alerted India to the fact that Russia had begun to treat India and Pakistan on a parity basis. Moreover, India learned that Pakistan had started receiving military aid from Russia soon after the Tashkent meeting. That all this was related to the growing hostility between China and Russia was no comfort to India. Mrs. Gandhi therefore sought and received assurances that the Soviet Union would not befriend Pakistan at the cost of Indian interests.

Two events in 1971 made a deeper mark on Indian foreign policy than even the 1962 Chinese invasion. One was the signing of a security pact between India and the Soviet Union in August, 1971. The other was the Indo-Pak war in December, 1971, which resulted in the breakup of Pakistan and the birth of Bangladesh.

The Indo-Soviet "Treaty of Peace, Friendship and Cooperation," signed by both parties on August 9, 1971, was a product of compelling circumstances; the timing of the event bears witness to this. It is now known that the Soviets had been encouraging India since 1969 to execute an agreement of this order. The hangup of nonalignment or the fear of alienating the U.S.A. may have prevented India from agreeing to this commitment earlier, but a quick reading of developments on the subcontinent of South Asia between March and August, 1971, convinced India that if she did not accept the treaty then she would suffer a strategic setback far worse than what she faced in 1962.

In March, 1971, political developments in the two wings of Pakistan culminated in a civil war between East and West Pakistan. Troops from West Pakistan were dispatched to control the situation in the Eastern wing and to suppress the movement for a separate and free state of Bengali-speaking Muslims. Freedom forces in the East conducted a highly successful guerilla campaign against the West Pakistani army. As the situation escalated into a full scale war between Pakistani troops and Mukti Bahini, the Bengali freedom force, millions of terror-stricken East Pakistanis fled to the neighboring state of West Bengal in India. The influx of nearly 10 million refugees at its peak created an untenable economic problem for India. Appeals from India to the United Nations and the major powers failed to correct the situation. At the same time the brutal suppression of the Bengalis in East Pakistan generated a tremendous pressure on India for recognition of a Free Government of Bangladesh and intervention by the Indian army on behalf of forces of liberation.

While Prime Minister Gandhi was caught in the dilemma, some more disturbing news surfaced. President Nixon had indicated to the Indian Government that the U.S.A. did not wish to see India involved in something that was strictly an internal affair of Pakistan. He further asserted that the United States was putting pressure on General Yahya Khan, president of Pakistan, to make peace with the East Bengalis. Nixon, however, had no immediate solution for the millions of refugees. Worse still in India's eyes was the U.S. government's continued supply of arms to Pakistan.

India was stung by these reports. But one more surprise had yet to unfold. President Nixon's foreign policy advisor Henry Kissinger visited New Delhi prior to his secret trip to Peking via Islamabad, the capital of Pakistan, to arrange for a meeting between President Nixon and Chairman Mao Tse-tung. When in New Delhi, Kissinger is reported to have told Indian officials that "if China entered the fray between India and Pakistan, India must not expect any help from the U.S."[3] The same warning was given to India's ambassador L. K. Jha in Washington by U.S. Secretary of State William Rogers. Soon thereafter, news surfaced that Nixon and Mao would meet in Peking in early 1972. These related facts meant one thing for India—the United States had thrown her lot with Pakistan and China. It was certain that if events forced India to intervene in East Pakistan to protect Indian interests, China and the U.S. could be expected to come to Pakistan's aid. India had only one way out. She could sign the pact with Russia which despite Soviet pressure, India had spurned up to that point.

Given the circumstances, India took the initiative by secretly sending her former ambassador to Russia, D. P. Dhar, to Moscow for talks. This was soon followed by the arrival of Soviet Foreign Minister Andre Gromyko in New Delhi on August 8. The next morning it was revealed to the world that India and the USSR had signed a treaty of friendship. Regardless of the title used, certain clauses of the treaty made it clear that it was a defense pact. For example, article IX says:

> In the event of either Party being subjected to an attack or a threat thereof, the High Contracting Parties shall immediately enter into mutual consultations in order to remove such threat and to take appropri-

ate effective measures to ensure peace and the security of their countries.⁴

Space limitations do not permit a full discussion of the treaty here. Suffice it to say that for the first time India had taken a step to strengthen her military capability through an alliance with one of the two superpowers. The long range repercussions of this action are yet to unfold, but India soon realized the immediate benefits of the pact.

Under the orders of the then Pakistani President, General Yahya Khan, elections were held in West and East Pakistan in December, 1970, to elect representatives to the National Assembly, which was to draft a new constitution for the country. Under universal suffrage, which the president granted to the surprise of many, the results were highly upsetting for him. The Awami League Party, led by Sheikh Mujiber Rahman from East Pakistan scored a resounding victory. It won 167 seats as opposed to a total of 146 seats won by the other ten parties put together. With nearly two-thirds of the country's population living in East Pakistan, this was to be expected. But it was most unnerving for the president because Mujiber Rahman's party had secured its smashing success on a platform that called for greater political and economic independence for the eastern wing of Pakistan. Sheikh Mujib sought a federal constitution which, while giving complete control to the center in defense and foreign affairs, left all the residual power with the federating states of East and West. He wanted economic, fiscal, and legal reforms which would eliminate the stark economic disparities between the two parts of Pakistan.

The Sheikh's demands were not surprising. Ever since the creation of Pakistan, ruling power over the country had rested with the West. Early prime ministers and then the two military leaders came from West Pakistan; 94 percent of the Civil Services personnel, 85 percent of the Foreign Service personnel and 95 percent of the Army personnel came from West Pakistan.

On the economic side, while the eastern wing provided 75 percent of the export and foreign earnings, it was allotted only 25 percent of the imported goods. With less than 40 percent of the population, the western wing received 77 percent of all developmental funds, with the result that industry was concentrated in the West, and the East provided all the raw materials. Per capita income in the West was nearly 60 percent higher than in the East.

Even though at the time of the birth of Pakistan, the two parts were considered as one because Islam was the common religion of the vast majorities of the peoples in the East and West, before long it had become clear that ethnically and culturally the two wings were as far apart as the thousand mile distance that separated them geographically. The dominant Punjabis, as well as the other West Pakistani ethnic groups, felt distinctly superior to the mild-mannered Bangali-speaking East Pakistani.

The results of the December, 1970, elections thus carried an alarming and ominous message for President Yahya Khan. He announced on March 1, 1971, that convening of the National Assembly was postponed indefinitely. Succeeding events came quickly in the aftermath of this announcement. Riots broke out all over East Pakistan, and troops from West Pakistan were dispatched to bring the situation under control. While Yahya Khan made surface attempts to negotiate with the popular leader Sheikh Mujib, the Pakistani army in the name of law and order resorted to strong-arm tactics as Martial Law prevailed all over the land. On March 26, 1971, Sheikh Mujiber Rahman proclaimed the independence of East Pakistan at Dacca, the capital city, giving birth to the Free State of Bangladesh. He was immediately arrested. But the people of Bangladesh responded to his call for independence, and the Pakistani army had a full-scale revolution on its hands.

Forces of Mukti Bahini, the revolutionary force consisting of defecting soldiers, students, workers, and peasants, were no match for the regular Pakistani troops, which were now being reinforced with men and materiel. But the army from West Pakistan was in addition facing a hostile and determined population of nearly 70 million. Under these conditions, Mukti Bahini made it impossible for Yahya's troops to succeed in imposing total control. Frustrated in their attempt to crush the uprising, Pakistan's soldiers ruthlessly killed civilians as well as soldiers.

As cited earlier scores of refugees began to cross the border into India. As their numbers climbed into millions, India turned to the world and appealed for immediate help to solve a situation that promised to become uglier by the hour. The general response of the nations was to caution India against the temptation of intervening in an affair that they maintained was purely an internal problem of Pakistan. Nations were prepared to send food and clothing for refugee relief, but expected that once the situation in Pakistan had settled down, the refugees would be welcomed back to their homes. India could draw little comfort from such response.

When the General Assembly of the United Nations met in September, 1971, all its members were fully informed about the situation on the South Asian subcontinent. They knew that millions of refugees now in India could not return to their homes as long as the Pakistani army continued to occupy East Bengal. They also knew that a stage had been reached where no solution that did not grant self-rule to the people of Bangladesh could bring peace and stability to the subcontinent.

The various resolutions introduced in the Assembly not only fell short of the mark, but pointed to the ever-present fear of all member nations: No nation wants the U.N. to meddle in its internal affairs. Yet there is only a thin line that divides a domestic upheaval from a threat to international peace.

Some Western countries proposed that U.N. observers be posted on both sides of the Indo-Pak border. The proposal failed because India refused to permit any foreign observers on her soil. U.N. Secretary General U Thant asked the Security Council to debate the Pakistan request that U.N. observers be posted on the East Bengal border. This was rejected by both India and Bangladesh, because they interpreted this move as an attempt on the part of Pakistan to blow up the issue as a conflict between India and Pakistan, and turn the attention away from the struggle for self-rule. No resolution was introduced in the Security Council or the General Assembly to take note of the atrocities committed by Pakistani troops. No pressure was applied to persuade either side to reach a compromise.

Thus while the nations of the world watched, the refugee problem and the demand on the part of the Indian people and Parliament to recognize Bangladesh and send the Indian army to the aid of Mukti Bahini, increased tensions between India and Pakistan.

On December 3, 1971, the Pakistan air force launched a simultaneous attack on several Indian airfields located not far from the western India-Pakistan border. This was followed by a formal declaration of war against India by Pakistan. Prime Minister Gandhi responded by putting the country on war footing. On December 6, India granted recognition to the People's Republic of Bangladesh. Diplomatic relations between India and Pakistan snapped the same day.

This was the third war between India and Pakistan. The 1948 conflict was confined to the Kashmir front and ended in a stalemate. The 1965 clash was on two fronts, Kashmir and the western border; this too ended in a draw. The 1971 confrontation, an all out war on all fronts, was basically being fought to decide whether the nation of Pakistan would survive with two wings or whether its eastern wing would emerge as Bangladesh.

At the very outset two things were clear. Odds were never before as favorable to India as they were on this occasion. The August treaty with the Soviet Union had placed a check on both China and the U.S.A.; they would not intervene directly in behalf of Pakistan. Previously, the major powers had cut off military aid to pressure the two sides to cease fighting. This time the Soviet Union was pledged to continue to aid India, while China and the U.S. supplied the military equipment to Pakistan. In addition some 70 million East Bengalis were in revolt against their previous governors and sought the assistance of the Indian army to oust Pakistani troops from their soil. Small wonder that under these conditions India was determined that the outcome would not be another stalemate: It had to be a military and political victory.

The 14 day war between India and Pakistan ended on December 16, 1971, when the Pakistani Army surrendered unconditionally in Bangladesh. India declared a unilateral cease-fire on the western front on December 17. General Yahya Khan had no choice but to accept the fait accompli.

The impact of the war on Indian foreign policy was massive. The victory injected India with a sense of confidence, security, and self-reliance. The war affected her relations with many nations according to the manner in which they had responded to the hostilities. It placed Indo-Pak relations in an entirely new context.

When the hostilities ceased with the surrender of Pakistani troops in Bangladesh, India insisted that any permanent settlement of outstanding issues must be a result of bilateral talks between the two countries. She refused to accept any third nation intervention, and resisting extreme pressure from world powers, adamantly stuck to the position that 90,000 Pakistani prisoners of war would not be released without negotiations on associated matters.

Prime Minister Gandhi initiated the first summit meeting with Pakistan's new president Z. A. Bhutto in Simla, India, in June–July, 1972, to discuss and resolve outstanding issues.

The Simla Agreement signed by Prime Minister Gandhi and President Bhutto on July 3, 1972, was the beginning of an attempt by the two long-standing antagonists to put their relationship on a new footing in the aftermath of the 14 day war. Both sides agreed "that the basic issues and causes of conflict which have bedeviled the relations between these countries for the last 25 years shall be resolved by peaceful means." It was also agreed that differences would be settled through bilateral negotiations, without any involvement of an outside power.

To restore and normalize relations between the two countries step by step, the agreement called for a move toward resumption of communications in all areas, including overflights. It enjoined the two parties to start the process of withdrawing their respective forces to their side of the international border, which was accomplished in the following month of December. And the agreement further stated that: "In Jammu and Kashmir the line of control resulting from the cease-fire of December 17, 1971, shall be respected by both sides without prejudice to the recognized position of either side."[5]

The Simla Agreement paved the way for further high level talks in July, 1973. These resulted in the second major agreement between the two countries, a three-way repatriation accord. The agreement sent back home 91,000 Pakistani POWs, as well as civilian internees, held in India since 1971. At the same time it called upon Pakistan to accept most of the 260,000 Pakistani nationals who were in Bangladesh and who desired to emigrate. Also, the agreement permitted all Bengalis stranded in Pakistan since the war, some 160,000 in number, to return to Bangladesh. Representatives of Bangladesh did not participate in the deliberations, but the final settlement was reached with the full consultation and concurrence of the Bangladesh government.

Finally in 1974, Pakistan recognized Bangladesh. No war crime trials were held against any of the Pakistani prisoners, as Bangladesh had earlier threatened. Before the year was out, India and Pakistan had reestablished travel and communication links. On November 30, 1974, the two countries signed a protocol which paved the way for resumption of trade between the two neighbors soon thereafter.

In a joint statement on May 14, 1976, the governments of India and Pakistan announced that diplomatic relations between the two states, severed in December, 1971, would be fully restored in the immediate future. During the following month the two countries reached agreement to resume air and rail traffic suspended in 1965. These were the most hopeful signs of progress on the road to normalization of relations.

While Mrs. Gandhi can thus claim to have significantly altered the state of relations with Pakistan, the situation is far from lasting stability. The Kashmir issue still remains a bone of contention. India's nuclear blast drew the loudest protest from Pakistan. Her representative has placed a proposal before the United Nations seeking to establish a nuclear free zone in South Asia. India has opposed it on the grounds that any projected nuclear free zone not applicable to the whole of Asia—especially China—would be discriminatory. Pakistan's proposal is obviously directed against India.

In the absence of her own nuclear power ability, Pakistan is convinced that only resumption of large scale American military aid will give her protection against India's power and possible coercion. Prime Minister Bhutto made a strong bid for arms assistance on his trip to Washington, D.C., in February 1974. In a countermove, India's foreign minister, Y. B. Chavan, wrote to Secretary of State Henry Kissinger that any American arms supplies to Pakistan would disrupt the process of normalization now under way. Chavan added that this could "adversely affect the sincere efforts of India to set its relations with the U.S.A. on a mature and constructive basis."[6]

On February 24, 1975, the United States announced its decision to resume the sale of arms to Pakistan. India viewed this as a great setback for Indian foreign policy and Indo-Pak relations. Mrs. Gandhi, commenting on Indo-Pak relations in December, 1974, said: "Sometimes we go a little forward. Then it looks as though that we are going backwards, because across the border all kinds of statements are made which are quite provocative even though we don't reply in kind."[7]

India and Bangladesh

The emergence of East Pakistan as the free state of Bangladesh is a plus for Indian foreign policy under the stewardship of Prime Minister Gandhi. Long-standing hostility between India and Pakistan made it necessary for India to assume that she was threatened by Pakistan on two fronts, a problem that assumed grave proportions after 1962. As China and Pakistan began to close ranks in the 1960s, India feared that China could be permitted to use East Pakistan as the stage for creating overt action or internal disorder in India. While such a contingency never materialized, India expected the worst from both quarters. Any danger of this nature seems to have been eliminated.[8]

The birth of Bangladesh has destroyed Pakistan's claim that the Muslims of the subcontinent feel more secure under Pakistani rule because she is constitutionally a Muslim state. It has weakened Pakistan's claim over Kashmir, for it was always assumed in many Western quarters that since the majority of Kashmiris are Muslim, it is therefore in the interest of the people that the territory belong to Pakistan.

Inasmuch as India made a total commitment to the cause of the liberation movement, India feels she can depend upon the goodwill and gratitude of the leadership of Bangladesh for many years to come. Given the nature of nation states, however, there is no guarantee that this pattern of relationship will endure indefinitely.

Bangladesh's massive economic problems have already raised some issues. She must go beyond India to search for economic assistance. India's own economy is in distress; she can hardly begin to attack the enormous problems of her neighbor. If Bangladesh comes to rely heavily on a major power for her economic viability, India would watch this development very carefully. Seeds of possible future friction are inherent in this situation.

The issue of large-scale smuggling operations on the border of the two countries has already created some irritation in Dacca as well as New Delhi. There have been border skirmishes between the troops of the two countries. It was expected that free Bangladesh and India would become very active trading partners; this has not so far materialized. Allocation of waters from the two eastern rivers, the Ganges and the Brahmaputra, to satisfy the needs of both countries is a sensitive and critical issue. No easy solution is in sight, even though both sides show confidence that they will come up with a satisfactory answer before long.

Warning voices are being raised in Bangladesh about Indian domination. Certain segments have openly shown concern that Pakistani control might be replaced by Indian control. Pakistan's Prime Minister Bhutto in his recent trip to Bangladesh, first since the inception of the new state, voiced hopes that the old relationship between the two could be restored, on a basis of complete equality. There are signals that as the euphoria of victory against Pakistan fades, a foundation of common economic and strategic interest will have to be built as a guarantee for lasting friendship.

India-Bangladesh relationships changed slightly with the death of Sheikh Mujiber Rahman. Sheikh Mujib was assassinated and his government overthrown in an army take-over on August 15, 1975. The new government contained most of the previous cabinet but was considered less pro-Indian than Mujib's regime. A counter-coup took place on November 5. While it is believed that this government will follow a line very close to that of Mujib, the events have created an unsettling effect which will take time to fade. The present government has assured India that Bangladesh will continue to abide by all bilateral and international agreements entered into while Mujib was in power. Nonetheless, it is apparant that in the absence of that bond of mutual trust which prevailed between the leadership of the two countries in the days of the Sheikh, relations between India and Bangladesh will rest on uncertain ground for some time to come.

India cannot afford to see any hostile regime assume power in Bangladesh. On the other hand no regime in Bangladesh will survive politically if it accepts the status of a satellite state. Presently, India is maintaining a very low profile in Bangladesh, observing every caution not to lend credence to those few voices shouting against Indian domination. India's diplomatic skill will be tested to its fullest in the coming years in her efforts to maintain a close ally on her eastern border.

India and the Middle East

The Kashmir issue has been a dominant note in India's foreign policy toward the Middle East since 1948. Concerned that Muslim nations would support Pakistan as a solid bloc, the Indian government did not extend full recognition to the newly-founded state of Israel. In the years since, diplomatic relations between India and Israel have never reached the embassy level.[9]

India was concerned when Iran, Iraq, Pakistan, and Turkey became parties to the security treaty, known as the Baghdad Pact,[10] in October, 1955. The pact was injurious to India's interests because it carried the implication that the Muslim members of the treaty would come to Pakistan's aid in case of an Indo-Pak confrontation. Also the treaty offended the concept of nonalignment espoused by Nehru, since it had been inspired by the U.S.A. as an anticommunist move, and Britain and France were the other members of the pact.

But India took comfort that she had developed a close relationship with Egypt under Nasser. President Nasser made common cause with Nehru in advocating a posture of nonalignment for the Afro-Asian world. Nasser was determined to remove the dominant Western influence from the Middle East. While he became the chief spokesman for the Pan-Arab movement, he strongly opposed the formation of a Pan-Islamic movement.

India reciprocated Egypt's goodwill on every possible occasion. Nehru was in the forefront fighting for Egypt's cause when the 1956 Suez crisis erupted. In the United Nations, India cast her vote with the Arab states on every conflict with Israel. In fact, this unequivocal support of the Arab cause was seriously questioned in the Indian Parliament, as the attitude of certain Arab states was considered to be anti-Indian. In the Indo-Pak war of 1965, most of the Arab states expressed support for Pakistan. India, with more than 60 million Muslims, was not allowed to participate in the Muslim nations' conference at Rabat in 1969. During the same year, however, when Hindu-Muslim riots broke out in one of the Indian cities, the King of Saudi Arabia sent a message to Mrs. Gandhi registering protest and displeasure on behalf of Muslim nations. In the Indo-Pak war of 1971, Iran and Jordan supplied fighter planes to Pakistan with the acquiescence of the United States.

However, events unfolding in the aftermath of the Arab-Israeli war in 1973 set a new tone for India's relations with the countries of the Middle East. The Arab states put together a solid front to compel Israel, and her staunch ally the United States, to accept certain conditions to bring peace to the Middle East and to settle the issue of Palestinian refugees. They threatened to withhold oil supplies to the Western world if the U.S. and Israel failed to respond. The energy crisis of 1974 had a near-crippling effect on world economy. The United States felt its shock: Her leaders issued a warning that any attempt on the part of the oil-producing countries to strangle the economy of the Western world would force the U.S. to take strong countermeasures. In turn the Arab states proclaimed that they would not be intimidated and would pursue an independent course. The Arab world began uniting the non-Western nations behind its cause. On her return from a trip to Iraq in January 6, 1975, Mrs. Gandhi told reporters that "Iraq and other Gulf countries were very much worried about the U.S. threat to oil-producing states."[11] These developments worked to India's benefit.

Also, with the wide acceptance of Bangladesh as an independent entity, the myth was broken that Pakistan was the sole protector of Islam on the subcontinent. India's detonation of a nuclear device in 1974 provided one more incentive for improved relations. The test demonstrated that India was highly advanced in nuclear technology. The Middle Eastern states could draw upon this reservoir of India, if they so desired. On the other hand India's need for oil was critical. The combined effect of all these happenings brought India dividends for her long pursued pro-Arab policy.

During 1974 and early 1975 mutual exchanges of visits took place between India and many of the oil-producing nations. Aside from the goodwill generated by these visits, they also resulted in some significant agreements.

India and Iran

Prime Minister Gandhi visited Iran in April, 1974. The Shah of Iran returned this visit in October, 1974. At a press conference in New Delhi on October 3, 1974, the Shah said that "firm friendship with India" ruled out any arms aid to Pakistan, "if they start an aggressive war on India." He also expressed the view that arms aid would not serve the interest of establishing peace on the subcontinent.[12]

India and Iran signed several agreements relating to economic cooperation during the Shah's visit. One of the major agreements called for collaboration to set up an aluminum plant, an iron ore extraction facility, and a joint shipping line. The Shah stated that his country's financial participation in various joint projects with India would eventually amount to a billion dollars.

On the question of whether India could assist Iran in her plans to develop nuclear power generation, the Shah said: "Once we start our nuclear energy programs to produce electricity and even before, we can hold discussions with India on all pertinent subjects."[13]

A technical team headed by Iran's deputy minister of labor, Dr. F. Nasseri, arrived in New Delhi in January, 1975, to discuss arrangements to secure technical personnel from India in the fields of engineering, transport and construction, and other areas.

India and Iraq

Vice-President Saddam Hossain of Iraq visited India in March, 1974. India's prime minister paid a return visit in January, 1975. Subsequent to her visit it was announced that Iraq would supply India with 2.8 million tons of oil in 1975. Iraq's minister of information, Tarig Aziz, told the press that the two countries were putting together an agreement whereby India would possibly become a continued supplier of iron ore and aluminum to Iraq. He said Iraq would finance the expansion of Indian facilities for manufacture of pelletized ore for sponge iron production in Iraq. He also held out the possibility that India would secure credit to purchase oil from Iraq.[14]

India and Libya

In October, 1974, an agreement was signed permitting India to explore oil in Libya. The two states will share the resulting production. Also under the agreement India will train a number of Libyan technicians. The agreement allows India to explore the possibility of exchanging Libyan crude oil for fertilizers.

India and the Sudan

An agreement covering the fields of science and economics was signed by India and the Sudan on November 28, 1974. The agreement calls on India to conduct studies with the aim of establishing cement, textile, and sugar industries in the Sudan in the near future. The extent of India's input in establishing the industries will be determined by feasibility studies. India has agreed to supply the equipment on a deferred payment basis at the initial stages. The final arrangements will be worked out when the feasibility reports become available.

India and Saudi Arabia

Sheikh Ahmed Yamani, the petroleum minister of Saudi Arabia, visited New Delhi for three days in February, 1975. During his stay he explored the possibilities of Indo-Saudi cooperation in economic and scientific fields. Before leaving New Delhi, he agreed to set up a joint commission to investigate the feasibility of collaboration between India and Saudi Arabia in the manufacture of such items as drugs and fertilizers. While maintaining that Saudi Arabia would not extend a preferential oil price or credit to purchase oil to India or any other developing state, he announced that his country was willing to grant India long-term easy credit for the purposes of starting joint industrial projects which could be located in either country.[15]

India and Afghanistan

India's policy of friendship toward Afghanistan continues, as it has always held a special significance for India. This Muslim state, bordering the northwestern frontiers of Pakistan, supports and encourages the Pushtu-speaking peoples in the borderland who are in revolt against the government in Islamabad and seek self-rule. While India has refrained from any direct involvement in this area, she has cultivated the friendship of the Afghans. It has always been comforting for India to know that unsettled conditions in borderlands immediately to the west of Pakistan remain a constraint upon Pakistan.

* * *

By no means do the above accounts cover all of India's recent activities in the Middle East, but they do show that India's access to the leadership of the major states in the region has increased. Adroitly cultivated, India's influence could become more effective and widespread. Her economic ties will prove highly beneficial. But more than that, India's close relationship with some of the key states would guarantee a secure western border despite continuing friction with Pakistan. In January, 1975, when India recognized the Palestine Liberation Organization as the agency which represents the legitimate aspirations of the Palestinian refugees, it was one more sign that India was searching for a new regional partnership to guarantee subcontinental stability and order.

India and the Himalayan Border States

The Communist takeover on the Chinese mainland in 1949 caused India, in the interests of her security, to become involved in the internal and external affairs of Bhutan, Sikkim, and Nepal, states on the northern frontier between India and China.

India and Bhutan

During the British rule, relations between India and Bhutan were guided by the 1910 treaty of Punakha. Under this treaty the British retained total control of Bhutan's foreign relations, but left her free to manage her own internal affairs. In August, 1949, at the initiative of the Nehru government, a new treaty was executed to establish relations between free India and Bhutan. The main features of this Treaty of Perpetual Peace and Friendship are the same as that of the treaty of Punakha: "The Government of India undertakes to exercise no interference in the internal administration of Bhutan. On its part the Government of Bhutan agrees to be guided by the advice of the Government of India in regard to its external relations." But whereas the British not only "guided" but dictated Bhutan's foreign policy, India has had to pursue a more diplomatic course to achieve similar results.

When China occupied Tibet in 1950, Bhutan was alarmed; as a result she cultivated close ties with India. But Bhutan refused to accept major economic aid from India for a long time. No Indian troops were ever stationed in Bhutan as a security measure.

In 1959 when friction between China and India became apparent, Bhutan agreed, at the urging of Nehru, to the building of a road link between India and Bhutan. Plans were also drawn at this time which would permit the Indian army to come to Bhutan's assistance in case of an emergency. Nehru made a statement in the Lok Sabha on August 28, 1959, indicating how India felt about the border states. He said:

> ... Our position is quite clear. The Government of India is responsible for the protection of the borders of Sikkim and Bhutan and of the territorial integrity of these two states and any aggression against Bhutan and Sikkim will be considered as aggression against India.[16]

Sino-Indian confrontation in 1962 did not lead to Chinese incursions into Bhutan. Nonetheless, the event cemented relations between India and Bhutan. No Bhutanese ruler has challenged India's right to guide the kingdom's external relations. Despite all attempts by China to deal with Bhutan directly, she has refused to establish a direct dialogue, instead dealing with China through India. On India's part, she has never found it necessary to intervene in Bhutan's internal affairs. Also, India has cooperated in securing for Bhutan membership in international organizations, sponsoring Bhutan's membership in the Colombo Plan in 1962. In 1969 Bhutan joined the Universal Postal Union, the only agency with which she is associated outside the General Assembly. Bhutan was admitted to the U.N. General Assembly in September, 1971, with India's support and blessings. Bhutan thus retains the sense of sovereignty she seeks. At the same time India's leadership seems firm in its resolve that no alien forces will be allowed to take hold in Bhutan.

India and Sikkim

Sikkim is situated at the edge of the direct and accessible route from Tibet to the plains of India. Therefore, it has held strategic significance for independent India, and British India before it. During the British rule Sikkim was a protectorate with a status similar to that of the princely states of India. Britain and China signed treaties in 1890 and 1893 that recognized Britain's protective shield over Sikkim. The king of Sikkim, called the Chogyal, sat in the Chamber of Princes with the other heads of the princely states in India. The British Viceroys of India used this assembly to dictate the major policies which the princes were obliged to observe. The British thus had total control over the internal and external policies of Sikkim, unlike Bhutan and Nepal.

In 1947 India assumed that the same rights over Sikkim as existed under the presence of the British were now India's. Nehru did not move to call for accession of Sikkim to India as he did with the other princely states. But changing circumstances made it necessary that free India and Sikkim formalize their relationships.

The Government of India announced in June, 1949, that it was taking over the administration of the state of Sikkim at the request of the Chogyal. The King had invited India when he found that public agitation against his rule made it impossible for him to administer the state. On December 5, 1950, India and Sikkim signed the Treaty of Perpetuity which enjoined that Sikkim was to be a Protectorate of India. Sikkim was given full autonomy in internal affairs, but the state's defense and foreign affairs were placed squarely in Indian hands. The treaty stated that "the Government of Sikkim shall have no dealings with any foreign power." It also stipulated that India would have the "exclusive right of constructing, maintaining and regulating the use of railways, aerodromes and landing grounds and air navigation facilities, posts, telegraphs, telephones and wireless installations in Sikkim."[17] India was also given exclusive rights to "contract and maintain in Sikkim roads for strategic purposes and for the purpose of improving communications with India."[18]

After the 1962 border war with China, the Government of India became ever more conscious that Sikkim was vital to Indian defense. King Palden Thondup Namgyal inherited the throne in December, 1963. He and his American wife, New York socialite Hope Cook, decided to introduce social and political changes with the intent of bringing the tiny Himalayan principality into the twentieth century. They also sought to change the Indo-Sikkimese relationship. The Chogyal made public pronouncements that Sikkim must assume a status similar to that of Nepal and Bhutan. He made attempts to secure a seat in the U.N. through the efforts of outside powers. While these moves did not appeal to India, she refrained from taking any drastic steps. In April, 1973, however, Sikkim was caught in another administration crisis similar to the one that erupted in 1949. Demonstrations and rioting by the Nepali-speaking majority, who constitute more than 70 percent of the population but were never participants in the decision-making process, produced a state of chaos. On April 5, in a letter to the Indian Political Officer, K. S. Bajpai, the Chogyal requested the help of the Indian army in the interest of "public security." India assumed the responsibility for law and order and internal administration in Sikkim by an agreement between the King and the Indian government. On May 8, a tripartite agreement was signed by the Chogyal, India's Foreign Secretary Kewal Singh, and leaders of the three political parties of Sikkim. This constitutional agreement provided for the election of a popularly elected parliament with all the powers of law making, with universal suffrage. The Chogyal was made a constitutional monarch under the new management.

In July, 1974, the popularly elected National Assembly of Sikkim moved to request the Indian Parliament to make Sikkim a part of the Indian Union, while permitting the state to retain its distinct identity. In September the Indian Parliament adopted a constitutional amendment, which for all practical purposes makes Sikkim a part of the Indian territory. The Constitution Amendment Bill passed by the Indian Parliament and ratified by the requisite number of state legislatures in February, 1975, moved Sikkim from the status of a protectorate to an associate of the Indian Union. Under the new law Sikkim will send one representative to the lower house of the Indian Parliament, elected directly by the people, and one to the upper house chosen by the Sikkim Assembly.

Chogyal protested, but his people seemed to approve India's action. Nepal and Bhutan did not raise any objections, even if they were unhappy over the developments. China and Pakistan accused India of expansionism, but their attempts to raise the issue at the United Nations failed. India was confident that she had acted in accordance with the wishes of the people of Sikkim and the obligations of her treaty rights, and had reacted boldly and unhesitatingly to a situation involving her own security.

India and Nepal

Nepal is the largest of the buffer states between India and China. Ever since the Chinese occupation of Tibet, India's security considerations have become inextricably tied to Nepal's security and stability. More than that, because of its independent character, Nepal has become the center of Sino-Indian attention as well as Sino-Indian rivalry.

Nehru said to the Indian Parliament on December 6, 1950, that India appreciated Nepal's independence but could not "... allow anything to go wrong in Nepal or permit that barrier to be crossed or weakened, because that would be a risk to our own security."[19] Despite such affirmations, however, India has not been able to control Nepal as she does Bhutan or Sikkim. India has courted Nepal with economic aid and other assistance to make certain the state remains neutral in her policies toward India and China. India also wants to be sure that Nepal will not permit China to use Nepalese territory for anti-Indian activities.

The British accepted Nepal as an independent entity, but they dominated her foreign relations and trade. Under the British-Nepali treaty of 1923, the British resident in Kathmandu exercised overwhelming influence over the Ranas, the dynastic rulers of Nepal.

In July, 1950, free India and Nepal signed a new treaty that superseded all previous arrangements. The treaty recognized the sovereign status of Nepal. It placed no mutual obligations except to say that the two parties would inform each other of "any serious friction or misunderstanding with any neighboring state."[20]

India, however, became involved in the internal politics of Nepal in 1950 when forces of insurrection overthrew the rule of the Ranas. The King took refuge in the Indian Embassy and was later flown to New Delhi. Nehru was able to mediate the dispute between various political factions of Nepal, the Ranas, and the King. In February, 1951, King Tribhuvan was installed in power with the help of India. It was assumed that the King would begin to introduce democratic rule in Nepal. This never materialized. But during King Tribhuvan's rule, relations between India and Nepal were quite close. India trained Nepal's security forces in the early 1950s. India supplied the men and material for building connecting roads and airfields. Furthermore, Nepal permitted India to post intelligence personnel on the border between Nepal and Tibet.

The situation changed in 1955 when Tribhuvan's son Mahendra came to power. Voices were being raised within Nepal that the growing influence of India in Nepalese affairs amounted to a compromise of the sovereign status. To check this compromise the new King turned toward China. Nepal and China established diplomatic relations in August, 1955. Following this, substantial economic aid agreements were signed between the two countries. Premier Chou En-lai visited Nepal in January, 1957, and April, 1960.

While these developments were disturbing for the Indian government, it was fearful that any measures it could take would worsen the situation and even result in a direct confrontation between China and India. New Delhi poured more economic aid into Nepal. There was an exchange of visits between the heads of state. But beyond that India could not exert greater pressure.

King Mahendra bowed to domestic political pressure and introduced parliamentary rule in February, 1959. But popular rule under Prime Minister B. P. Koirala of the Nepali Congress lasted only until December 15, 1960. On that day, through a royal proclamation, the King dismissed Nepal's first elected government and assumed all powers of administration. At the same time he assured the two powers on its northern and southern borders that Nepal's foreign policy would stay neutral.

The King's diplomacy proved effective. In the 1962 war neither China nor India violated Nepal's territory. Even in the aftermath, Nepal continued to draw economic aid from India and China, as well as the U.S. and the USSR. King Mahendra died in January, 1972.

Prince Birendra was formally anointed as the King in February, 1975. Maharaja Birendra is the absolute ruler in the tradition of his father and has so far demonstrated the ability to wield domestic and foreign policy with the same adroitness. As long as domestic stability prevails in Nepal, neither India nor China will dare to risk a change in their policy toward this buffer state.

Since 1950 no ruler has sought India's intervention in Nepalese politics to maintain his power. The fact is that King Mahendra was not only able to sustain his absolute rule, but by seeking

Chinese friendship in the 1950s he was also successful in brushing off any attempts by India to strengthen her presence in Nepal. The Nepali Congress, which drew support as well as inspiration from the Indian National Congress Party, failed to receive any backing from India after 1955 primarily due to the King's strong protests over Indian intervention. To avoid the possibility of the King becoming too friendly with China, the Government of India promised not to permit the use of Indian territory for any antimonarchy movement. India thus reconciled to accept assurances from Nepal that if India made no attempts to dominate the state, it would return the compliment by keeping China at bay. India's future policy toward Nepal will be determined by Birendra's ability to maintain domestic tranquility and international neutrality.

India and Sri Lanka (Ceylon)

Sri Lanka* occupies a unique position among India's immediate neighbors. The relations between the two are exceptionally cordial. Both preserve their respective freedom of action in international affairs. Yet the leadership in both countries has adopted an identical approach to almost all the major international issues. Neither considers the other a potential security threat or a rival for international influence. And the two states have successfully settled the outstanding disputes between them through peaceful negotiations. There was always the fear that the problem of Indians resident in Ceylon could cause serious friction between the two. The leadership on both sides has, however, shown patience, restraint, and the will to find a solution to differences arising out of conflict of interest. The result is that they appear to have stabilized their relations on a lasting basis.

India and Sri Lanka achieved independence at about the same time, 1947–48, from their common colonial master, the British. While culturally the Indians and the Sinhalese were no foreigners to each other and no economic concerns divided them, nationalism ran deep in both states. Thus no prospects for permanent ties surfaced at the dawn of independence. India opted for the status of a sovereign republic within the British Commonwealth. Sri Lanka accepted "Dominion Status," which meant that the British Monarch continued as the chief of state for Sri Lanka. Also, refusing to subscribe to Nehru's posture of nonalignment, Sri Lanka's policymakers signed a security pact with Great Britain in 1947. In fact there were voices in Sri Lanka which expressed fears of Indian dominance in South Asia. Nonetheless, India and Sri Lanka stood together in the U.N. in opposition to colonialism and racialism. They were equally vocal in support of U.N. recognition of mainland China. In 1961 Sri Lanka

*Sri Lanka was known as Ceylon until 1970.

backed India on the Goan issue. And in the aftermath of the Sino-Indian conflict of 1962, Sri Lanka called upon the six-power Colombo Conference to find a solution to the boundary dispute between the two Asian giants. But it was not until the 1970s that India and Sri Lanka were able to lay the foundation for lasting cooperation and friendship. It was the problem concerning the status of about one million Indians resident in Sri Lanka that prevented these two countries from forging close ties any earlier.

The Indian community in Sri Lanka consists mainly of descendants of South Indians who migrated to the island in the nineteenth and early twentieth centuries. They were the main source of labor for the rubber and tea plantations. In 1948 their number was approximately 950,000. Under the Indian and Pakistani Residents (Citizenship) Act of 1949, some 850,000 applied for Ceylonese citizenship. The then government of Sri Lanka accepted only 134,188 applications. It soon became clear that the restrictions surrounding the act were meant to encourage most of the migrant workers to return to Indian soil.

Nehru signed an agreement with his neighbor in 1954 to tackle the issue. No practical solution was realized, however, and as late as the early 1960s some 900,000 persons of Indian origin remained "stateless." Sri Lanka would not accord citizenship to them. India was not enthusiastic about adding huge numbers to her already bulging population. She maintained that Ceylonese citizenship was the birthright of the workers.

The overall foreign policy outlook of the Ceylonese government moved closer to that of the Indian government in the late 1950s. Ceylon abandoned her pro-Western stance and joined the nonaligned group of nations. The British naval base in Ceylon was closed. But the problem of the overseas Indians continued to simmer until October, 1964, when for the first time the two governments agreed to fix definite quotas for citizenship and repatriation. Under the arrangements accepted by Prime Minister Shastri of India and Prime Minister Sirimavo Bandaranaike of Ceylon, it was agreed that 525,000 of the 975,000 persons of Indian origin in Ceylon would be granted Indian citizenship and repatriated over the next 15 years. Ceylonese citizenship was to be granted to 300,000. It was decided that the future status of the remaining 150,000 would be the subject of a separate agreement.

The settlement did not become operative until late 1967. Nevertheless, it paved the way for progressive betterment of relations between India and Sri Lanka. There was a series of visits exchanged between Prime Minister Gandhi and Prime Minister Bandaranaike. India made a hearty response to Sri Lanka's request for military assistance in 1971, when rebellion in parts of the country threatened internal stability. And when Mrs. Bandaranaike visited India in January, 1974, two key agreements were executed which cemented the relationship between the two states.

A joint communique issued on January 29, 1974, announced that a final settlement had been reached concerning the future of the 150,000 persons of Indian origin who were not covered by the 1964 accord. Half of them were given Indian citizenship and repatriated, while the other half received Ceylonese citizenship. At the same time it was announced that a speedy decision would be made to demarcate the boundary between the two countries in the waters at Palk Straits.

In June, 1974, when the water boundary line was finally demarcated, the agreement also settled a claim that had been under dispute since 1910. India recognized Sri Lanka's ownership of the island of Kachchative. Mutually satisfactory provisions were made for navigation, pilgrimage, fishing, and mineral exploration rights of both parties in the area. This put an end to all old quarrels. It set a pattern which India's leadership hopes can be repeated in sorting out relations with other neighbors.

Notes

[1] The term neighbors is loosely used here. The scope of the book does not permit detailed discussion of relations with every neighbor. Also, relations with China are dealt with separately.

[2] At the time of partition all the Muslims did not opt for Pakistan. Many Hindus did not immediately leave for India. Today, more than 60 million Muslims continue to reside in secular India. Pakistan, whose state religion is Islam, has a Hindu population of 1.6%. (Europa Year Book, 1975.)

[3] *Time*, August 23, 1971, p. 7.

[4] N. M. Ghatate, ed., *Indo-Soviet Treaty* (Delhi: Indian Publishing House, 1972), p. 15.

[5] *The Statesman Weekly* (Calcutta), July 8, 1972.

[6] *The Statesman Weekly* (Calcutta), February 15, 1975.

[7] As quoted in *India News*, Embassy of India, Washington, D.C., December 13, 1974.

[8] It should be noted, however, that while the government of Bangladesh is not apt to permit the use of its territory by China for hostile activity, Bangladesh Maoists and the Naxalites of West Bengal in India both receive aid and inspiration from Peking. How far China will succeed in welding unity between these two groups, and thus exploit the situation, is difficult to predict at this point.

[9] In 1947 India was selected as a member of the eleven-nation committee designated by the United Nations to make recommendations on the future of Palestine following British withdrawal in August, 1948. India, Iran and Yugoslavia submitted a minority plan. This plan suggested the creation of a federated state with Jewish and Arab units enjoying local autonomy. The

plan also placed a limitation on Jewish immigration after 3 years. It was rejected by the General Assembly. India voted against the majority proposal which advocated partition and establishment of two separate states. It should be noted that there is an Israeli Consulate in Bombay.

[10] In 1959 Iraq withdrew from the pact. The rest of the members of the treaty changed its name to CENTO during the same year.

[11] *Statesman Weekly* (Calcutta), January 25, 1975.

[12] *Ibid.*, October 5, 1975.

[13] *Ibid.*

[14] *India News*, Embassy of India, Washington, D.C., January 31, 1975.

[15] *The Statesman Weekly* (Calcutta), February 15, 1975.

[16] Jawaharlal Nehru, *India's Foreign Policy* (New Delhi: The Publication Division, Government of India, 1961), pp. 338–39.

[17] *Foreign Policy of India: Texts of Documents 1947–59*, pp. 37–40, cited by Charles H. Heimsath and Surjit Mansingh in *A Diplomatic History of Modern India* (New Delhi: Allied Publishers, 1971).

[18] *Ibid.*

[19] *Jawaharlal Nehru's Speeches 1949–53*, p. 176.

[20] *A Diplomatic History of India*, p. 203.

8

India and the "Big Three" Powers

China in India's Foreign Policy

First contacts between India and China go back to ancient times. An active Buddhist movement in China was primarily responsible for the cultural relationship that developed between the two countries. And as Buddhism began to fade in India, contact between India and China also weakened.

The ancient relationship between the two countries was not renewed until the dawn of the twentieth century. The political leadership of China and India developed an attitude of sympathy for each other's cause in the 1920s. While neither was in a position to help the other toward their respective goals, the nationalist leadership in both countries watched with interest the political developments taking place in the other's country. Thus when Japan attacked China in 1937, the Indian National Congress Party expressed sympathy with the Chinese cause and sent a medical unit, as a token of the Congress Party's support.

Existing circumstances did not permit more intimate relations. Nehru made a brief trip to China in 1939 as a guest of

President and Madam Chiang Kai-shek. Similarly, the Generalissimo and Madam Chiang visited India for a few days in 1942. Chiang Kai-shek expressed himself in favor of India's independence. The "Quit India" resolution passed by the Indian Congress Party in 1942, calculated to overthrow British rule in India, made specific mention that there was no intent to weaken the defense effort of China. Aside from expressing mutual sympathy, the two countries had no opportunity to develop any real relations. If the Himalayas had prevented the growth of close contact before, India's colonial status and China's instability proved formidable barriers to the growth of any meaningful ties once the two countries had discovered each other anew.

Formal relations between India and China as independent nations were established for the first time in October, 1946. Soon thereafter both were engulfed in conditions of civil war. In one case the result was partition of the subcontinent; India and Pakistan emerged as two sovereign states. In the other case a powerful and disciplined regime, claiming communist philosophy as its base, took control of the Chinese mainland. So when on December 30, 1949, Nehru's government announced its recognition of the Mao regime, breaking all relations with Chiang Kai-shek who had now established nationalist headquarters in Formosa, India and China were meeting on a new footing—neither nation was very well acquainted with the political ambitions of the other.

Relations between the two countries were strained during the first few years after the People's Republic of China had been established. In October, 1949, when the Communist Party of India was engaged in intensive terroristic activities, Mao Tse-tung sent a message to Ranadive, the Secretary of the Party, wishing the Indian Communists speed in their attempts to liberate India, and expressing the hope that India would one day go the Chinese way. Similarly, prior to the Chinese attack on Tibet in 1950, the *New China News Agency* reported that the "Anglo-American imperialists and their running dog, Pandit Nehru, were plotting a coup in Lhasa for the annexation of Tibet."[1]

In March, 1950, Nehru expressed a desire before the Indian Parliament to sign a treaty of friendship with the new regime on mainland China. There was no response of any sort from Peking. When in December, 1952, India advanced certain proposals for a Korean truce, they were denounced by Peking in rather strong language.

The picture suddenly changed in 1953. The Peking regime agreed to a settlement in Korea in March, 1953, based mainly on proposals submitted by India in 1952 and denounced by China at that time. In October, 1953, the Chinese government accepted a suggestion by the Indian government to settle certain matters concerning Indian trade in Tibet. This was the first time India had approached China concerning Tibet subsequent to China's occupation, without incurring Chinese wrath.

In his opening speech before the Geneva Conference in April, 1954, Chou En-lai expressed regret that an important Asian country like India, devoted to world peace, could not be present at the Conference. On his return from Geneva, the Chinese Prime Minister paid a three day visit to New Delhi. Only a few months later Nehru returned the courtesy of the Chinese Premier by journeying to Peking for a visit that lasted twelve days. What was even more significant was that on April 29, 1954, the governments of India and China signed an "Agreement on trade and intercourse between the Tibet region of China and India." The preamble stated that the agreement was based on the principles of mutual respect for each other's territorial integrity and sovereignty, mutual nonaggression, mutual noninterference in each other's internal affairs, equality and mutual benefit, and peaceful coexistence. These five principles formed the most notable feature of the agreement, as Nehru himself said before the Indian Parliament, and later became the landmark of India's foreign policy under the name of *Panch Shila*.[2]

The year 1955 saw India and China closer to each other than ever before. Cultural exchanges between the two countries and missions of goodwill surpassed all previous records. At the Bandung Conference India took great pains to establish that India and China could share the leadership of the Asian-African world. In the United Nations, India worked relentlessly for recognition of the mainland regime as the legitimate government of China.

The spirit of Panch Shila did not last long. The issue that gave yet another twist to Sino-Indian relations was supposed to have been resolved in the very agreement that contained the substance of Panch Shila. In signing the 1954 Agreement, Nehru abdicated all Indian rights in Tibet that had been transferred to independent India at the departure of the British. The Indian prime minister had bent over backwards to accommodate China in the hope that her lasting friendship would be secured. This gesture was calculated not only to solve the thorny situation in Tibet, but in addition to establish a feeling of mutual trust and understanding, guaranteeing settlement of any future issue without friction or rivalry. As later events proved, these were strictly one-sided assumptions. China entertained no such illusions.

The Tibetan problem erupted with renewed fury in 1959. Nehru revealed in Parliament on March 30, 1959, that India had known for two or three years that trouble was brewing within Tibet.

The sporadic fighting between the Tibetans and the Chinese all through this period mushroomed into a major Tibetan revolt on March 10, 1959. In detailing the events in Tibet, Nehru observed that there was a deep feeling of cultural kinship between the people of India and Tibet, and that his sympathies were with the Tibetan people.[3]

India granted political asylum to the Dalai Lama, who fled Lhasa on March 31. In granting asylum to the ruler of Tibet, India let it be known that he would not be surrendered to the Chinese government under any circumstances.[4]

Chinese response was quick. Indian traders in Tibet were harrassed by the Chinese authorities. The Chinese unilaterally declared that the Indian rupee would not be accepted as legal tender in Tibet. And the Chinese authorities imposed restrictions on the movements of Indian nationals as well as Indian representatives in Tibet.

But even more alarming was the news that Nehru brought to the House of the People on August 28, 1959. During the preceeding two or three years there had been incidents of intrusion on India's northern border by Chinese troops. While the prime minister described most of these incidents as being of a minor nature, it soon became clear that India and China were involved in a serious boundary dispute which covered the entire 2,500 mile-long border between the two countries.[5]

Indian public opinion had been aroused over Chinese suppression of Tibet as well as over border clashes. But resentment boiled to a pitch at the news of a clash between Sino-Indian troops in October, 1959, in which the government reported nine Indian soldiers killed and ten captured by the Chinese. Even Nehru, who had been advocating restraint all along, could not help reacting forcefully. He accused the Chinese of "breach of faith." On November 27, he declared in the Lok Sabha that if the situation with China ever worsened, millions of Indians would have to change their lives and become a "nation in arms."

The period between October, 1959, and October, 1962, was marked by a series of diplomatic exchanges between India and China. While both nations made sharp remarks, each professed no intention of resort to arms to solve the now serious boundary dispute. Both sides proceeded silently to take steps to advance and firm their individual claims over the disputed territory. Slowly but surely it became clear that neither side was willing to give ground, for that would be read by the other party and the nations at large as a sign of weakness. Even though the Indian military appears to have realized that they could not meet a Chinese military challenge, the foreign policymakers on each side seemed determined to demonstrate to their people and the world that their cause was just and they had every intention of holding on to their claim at any cost.

Chinese Premier Chou En-lai, accompanied by his foreign minister, Marshal Chen-yi, came to New Delhi in April, 1960, presumably to attempt through direct negotiations to settle the conflict before it reached the point of no return. But while both sides continued to express hopes for a settlement, their background tactics and strategy clearly indicate that little effort was being made to prevent the boundary dispute from escalating into an armed conflict. Both sides were adamant in their claims; each side was convinced that it would prevail with a show of force but without an open military confrontation. Thus with the single determination to preserve their national image, India and China inched toward October 20, 1962, when the better trained, better supplied, better organized, more disciplined, and numerically superior Chinese army marched across the entire northern border into Indian territory.[6]

The campaign lasted for about a month, with an interval of lull, but it was clear from the very start that militarily speaking India was no match for China. It was a one-sided affair; the Indian army was completely routed. Chinese troops made deep thrusts into India on the entire front but especially in the northeast frontier area. "A shaken Krishna Menon (the defense minister), asked by the journalists where he thought the advancing Chinese could be stopped, said: 'The way they are going there is not any limit to where they will go.' "[7]

By all accounts India was totally unprepared for the Chinese attack.

> It has now been established beyond any doubt that both Nehru and Krishna Menon regarded . . . the Chinese moves and our countermoves in the form of establishing pickets in the forward areas as a game of chess. While the Chinese pickets in our territory were backed by a massive military build-up across the frontier, our pickets had no military support at all. Even Nehru's famous statement of 13 October 1962, in which he declared that Indian troops had been ordered to evict Chinese forces from Indian territory, resulted primarily from a disbelief in the possibility of any strong military action by China.[8]

China had planned well. She had no intention of creating a climate wherein the U.S. or other major powers would have the opportunity to hastily build up India's military strength. On November 21, 1962, China declared a unilateral cease-fire along the entire Sino-Indian border. She also announced that starting on December 1, 1962, the Chinese frontier guard would withdraw to positions 20 kilometers behind the line of actual control which existed between

China and India on November 7, 1959. India had no choice but to accept, with a great sense of relief, an outcome that China had imposed at the point of a gun. By bringing the war to a halt at a point when they could have marched with little challenge into the plains of India, the Chinese secured far greater gains than the mere resolution of the boundary dispute. China had carried out a successful punitive expedition and demonstrated that she desired to occupy no more territory than what was traditionally hers. She established her military superiority on the Asian scene. She destroyed the image of India as an Asian power, and India's role of leadership in Asia came to an end. Nehru felt greatly hurt that the Afro-Asian world he had championed in the corridors of the World Assembly responded with little sympathy in India's hour of distress.

But above all, in humiliating India, China had deflated the personal appeal and power of Nehru at home and abroad. For the first time in his life Nehru did not go unscathed by his Party and Parliament for what was apparently a major foreign policy blunder. He was compelled to fire his defense minister, Krishna Menon, and many a high-ranking general was forced to resign. Even though Nehru continued in power, formally, until his death in 1964, his spirit was broken; his dreams for a strong but not military-minded India, serving as a beacon of light for the weak and poor peoples and nations of the world, seeking to preserve ideals of democracy and peace, were shattered. His will could no longer lead or prevail. Indian foreign policy had been coerced to change direction by forces from outside.

After the Chinese had unilaterally declared a cease-fire, Nehru encouraged the UAR and Ceylon to attempt to find a solution to the Sino-Indian boundary dispute. Burma, Cambodia, Ceylon, Ghana, Indonesia, and the UAR met in Colombo, Ceylon in December, 1962. This six power conference produced what is now known as the "Colombo Proposals" to resolve the conflict. Repeated negotiations with China and India to work out a final draft acceptable to both sides ended in failure. At this point the Afro-Asian nations abandoned their efforts to bridge the gap between the two Asian rivals. Nehru's death in 1964 left the burden of the problem with the new prime minister, Lal Bahadur Shastri.

Shastri concentrated on building India's defense and finding a way to rapprochement with India's major antagonists, China and Pakistan. After China exploded a nuclear device in October, 1964, India became extremely concerned about China's future intentions vis-à-vis India. Interestingly, India's prime minister suggested that the superpowers provide a nuclear umbrella to protect India from any nuclear attack or coercion. At the same time, in every foreign policy statement, he attempted to convey to China that India was ready to resolve outstanding issues through renewed negotiations. He failed to make any headway.

When the Indo-Pak war broke out in 1965, India was apprehensive that China would use the occasion to strike again. China did issue an ultimatum of sorts to the Indian government, but failed to carry out the threat when Britain and the U.S. made it clear that intervention by China would result in countermeasures by the two Western powers.

Sino-Indian relations stood where they were until Mrs. Gandhi became the prime minister in 1966. She made no major moves during her first few years in power, but left no doubt that she was concerned about China's nuclear threat. Mrs. Gandhi refused to sign the nuclear nonproliferation treaty. She made it clear that as long as China remained hostile, India had to leave open the option to achieve nuclear capability.

Between March and December, 1971, India watched with concern China's reaction to the events taking place on the South Asian subcontinent. In April China issued a statement firmly supporting the actions of Pakistan's President Yahya's regime, condemning the free Bangladesh movement, and accusing India of expansionist tendencies. Additional statements charging India with intentions of breaking up Pakistan were issued in the following months. In November Pakistan's president dispatched a delegation to Peking headed by the then foreign minister, Z. A. Bhutto, presumably to ascertain how far China was prepared to support Pakistan in reestablishing her authority in East Pakistan. But as December approached it became apparent that even after Bhutto's visit, China was not prepared to make any commitments of direct involvement. In contrast with the events of 1965, China did not even threaten India with dire consequences, aside from virulent criticism. Due to the force of the Indo-Soviet Treaty, and possibly because of a desire to strike a posture of reconciliation as she prepared to enter the United Nations, China refrained from any serious involvement in another Indo-Pak conflict.

The restraint observed by China in 1965 and 1971 leads one to believe that she is not prepared to launch on a reckless course of confrontation. However, it is clear that on both occasions, had she intervened, China was faced with the prospect of involvement with a major power. The U.S. and Britain discouraged Peking from making a move in 1965, and the Soviet Union proved to be the constraint upon China in 1971.

India cannot on her own match the power of China. Prime Minister Gandhi has made several efforts to begin a dialogue with

China. The response thus far has been negative. This is not only disturbing for India's policymakers, it also confirms their fears that the Chinese threat of open hostilities and coercion remains alive.

Apparently, India hoped her explosion of a nuclear device would gain her that prestige which would possibly impress upon China the need to strike a rapprochement. But China was uniquely silent about the Indian explosion. Her lack of reaction carried the implication that China considered India's experiment inconsequential in terms of the power equation. China's nuclear capability, which includes hydrogen bomb warheads and IRBMs, is much more advanced than India's. China's silence also indicated that she had no intention of conferring upon India the attention that she sought by becoming the sixth member of the nuclear club.

There are no signs that Sino-Indian relations will improve radically in the near future. China is convinced that in the presence of the Indo-Soviet treaty, India is a partner in the Soviet Union's attempts to encircle China. India, for her part, believes that if China refuses to enter into negotiations to resolve outstanding problems, and continues to support Pakistan in her anti-Indian activities, there is no choice for India except to bolster her defense with the Indo-Soviet security treaty.

Recently Albania's request to be permitted to open a mission in New Delhi was seen as a hopeful note, since Albania is a close ally of China. But about the same time that India absorbed Sikkim into an associate Indian state, China accused India of expansionism. China also warned India to stop pressuring Nepal to pursue a more pro-Indian policy. The net effect was to confirm India's suspicions and fears about China.

The Indian government announced on April 15, 1976, that an ambassador would be assigned to Peking in the coming months. This is a bold step toward normalization of relations as the diplomatic exchange between the two countries has rested at the Chargè d'Affairs level since the 1962 conflict. However, it is too early to consider this move as holding much promise especially since there was no similar announcement from Peking that the level of their mission in New Delhi would be raised.

India and the Soviet Union

The Soviet Union did not directly or indirectly assist the Indian independence struggle, nor did she make any specific pronouncements or moves calculated to help the Indian cause. However, Soviet Russia by her very existence was considered a force against colonial rule in India. Moreover, the anti-imperialist slogans of the

USSR were interpreted as policy statements in support of those nations suffering under alien rule.

India was generally sympathetic toward the Soviet Union at the end of World War II. This should not be misconstrued to mean that India was in a mood to accept Communism or was prepared to come under the Soviet heel. On the contrary, India was eagerly looking forward to asserting her independence in every way, something which had been denied her for over a hundred years. Simply, at a time when world suspicions against the Soviet Union were on the rise, there existed in India goodwill toward the USSR with no backlog of bitterness or rivalry. Thus in April, 1947, when formal relations were established between the two countries, all indications were that India and the Soviet Union were headed for an era of friendship.

Representatives of the two countries closed ranks on many an issue in the United Nations in 1947. They opposed the Union of South Africa's move to annex South-West Africa. Mrs. V. L. Pandit, India's first ambassador to the U.N., gained strong support from the Soviet side in her case against South Africa's alleged discrimination against the people of Indian origin. Also, the Indians and the Soviets pushed hard in the Trusteeship Committee to liberalize the trusteeship agreements submitted by the administering powers. The number of times the two voted together raised the comment in U.S. circles that India was drawing close to the Soviet bloc.

However, such speculation was premature. Before 1947 ended, the cordiality between India and the Soviet Union evaporated. Pointed criticism of the Indian government and Indian leaders began to appear in the Soviet press and in Soviet writings. This continued for more than five years, despite India's open displeasure.

When Poland vacated a seat on the Security Council in October, 1947, there was a tussle between India and the Ukraine to procure that seat. India's reasons for wanting to gain that seat, as presented by Mrs. Pandit, were turned down and called irrelevant to the existing situation by Soviet Ambassador Andrei Vishinsky. Also, a few days later, India supported the adoption of the United States proposal for a "Little Assembly." Soviet Russia denounced the proposal as endangering world peace.

In the following years India and Soviet Russia found themselves on the opposite side on many an issue. Notable among these were the question of Ceylon's U.N. membership, the Dutch-Indonesian conflict, Korea, and Libyan independence.

In 1953, after the death of Stalin, Soviet policy assumed a new look. As a part of the overall change introduced by the new leadership, headed by Nikita Khrushchev, Indo-Soviet relations began to warm up again. The particular event that brought them close was the signing of the U.S-Pak security treaty in May, 1954. The military aid pact had the dual effect of alienating India against the Western powers while it spurred the Soviet Union to seek India's friendship. In order to prevent countries like India, Burma, and Indonesia from falling in line with Pakistan, the USSR not only sought to establish more cordial relations with these states but she also encouraged them in their posture of nonalignment.

The year 1955 opened with the signing of an agreement for the construction of a steel plant in India with Soviet help. Prime Minister Nehru was invited for a two-week visit to Moscow in June. Toward the end of the same year Soviet leaders Bulganin and Khrushchev returned the courtesy by visiting New Delhi. During their stay they made statements on Goa and Kashmir that proved to be a permanent Soviet commitment to support India's interests on these issues.

Moscow did not condemn Peking over the Sino-Indian war in 1962. But statements were made by the Soviet leadership implying that in their opinion China did not act prudently in crossing into Indian territory. In the 1965 Indo-Pak war Moscow adopted a neutral posture. But it was Soviet Premier Kosygin who finally brought together the leaders of the two warring states to work out their differences. During the 1960s India and the Soviet Union had very friendly relations. But both were cautious not to embrace each other. Their restraint ended in the 1970s.

India had been rudely awakened to the rising power of China in 1962; likewise, Sino-Soviet border clashes led to a new trend in Soviet Asian policy. Speaking before the World Communist Party Conference in Moscow in June, 1969, Party Chief Brezhnev remarked: "We are of the opinion that the course of events is also putting on the agenda the task of creating a system of collective security in Asia."[9]

India's reaction was not encouraging. Mrs. Gandhi said that "India would prefer a nonalliance security agreement composed of Asian states, guaranteed by both Russia and America."[10] India still believed that she was better protected against China when both superpowers applied the check. India was reluctant to become totally dependent upon either the U.S.A. or USSR. But the 1971 events closed the options for both India and the Soviet Union. The United States, anxious to strike a détente with China, put New Delhi and Moscow on guard. When the U.S. on the one hand armed Pakistan secretly and on the other hand conveyed to Mrs. Gandhi that a Chinese attack would not lead to U.S. intervention in India's behalf, the die had been cast. India and the Soviet Union signed the Treaty of Friendship and Cooperation in August, 1971, which has laid the basis for India's new approach in the search for strategic and economic security.

On December 5, the U.S. introduced a resolution in the U.N. Security Council which called upon India and Pakistan to cease hostilities and withdraw their armed forces to positions before the 1971 war began. Eleven members of the Security Council, including China, voted in favor of the resolution. Britain and France abstained. The Soviet Union vetoed it, as desired by India. Similar resolutions introduced on December 6 and 14 were also vetoed by the USSR.

In a statement issued from Moscow on December 5, Soviet official agency Tass placed the blame for the entire episode on the Government of Pakistan. It stated that:

> .... Since the Pakistani Government did not take measures for a political settlement in East Pakistan and continued to build up military preparations against India, the Soviet leaders informed President Yahya Khan that Pakistan's armed attack against India under whatever pretext would evoke the most resolute condemnation in the Soviet Union.... In the face of the military threat now hanging over Hindusthan, the Soviet Union calls for the speediest ending of the bloodshed and for a political settlement in East Pakistan on the basis of respect for the lawful rights and interests of its people. The Soviet Government also believes that the Governments of all countries should refrain from steps signifying in this or that way their involvement in the conflict and leading to a further aggravation of the situation in the Hindusthan Peninsula.[11]

To India, the Soviet response was most gratifying. Without question India could not have aided in the creation of Bangladesh in the absence of the Treaty of Friendship with the USSR.

On February 17, 1973, the Indo-Soviet Commission on economic, scientific, and technical cooperation, an offshoot of the Indo-Soviet Treaty, signed an elaborate protocol in New Delhi covering extensive areas of economic and technical assistance to India. According to this agreement, during the period of the "fifth plan," Russia will help India increase her production in such key fields as steel, nonferrous metals, oil refining, and exploration, chemicals and power generation, shipping and transport, and electronics.

Soviet Representative Skachkov observed at the time of signing the protocol that:

> ... 17 years ago the Soviet Union had helped only in setting up the Bhilai (steel) plant. Now, there were as many as 90 industrial and other projects in India which his country had helped to launch. Of these 50 were already in operation, though the capacity of some was not being fully realized.

He added:

> The Soviet-aided projects in India were the largest in any other part of the world, including Europe.[12]

India's Planning Minister, D. P. Dhar, remarked that:

> It was only natural that when the country was assessing the availability of resources for the Plan it should have consulted one of her greatest friends (the Soviet Union) to take a look at her capacity, her willingness and ability to help us in the successful completion of the aims and objectives set out in the plan. It was a matter of satisfaction that the Soviet Union had agreed to help us in the core sector of our industry, the development of which we consider to be of the very essence for bringing relief and succour to our teeming millions.[13]

Soviet Party Chief Brezhnev's visit to India in November, 1973, ended with a 15-year Indo-Soviet agreement for further development of economic and trade cooperation between the two countries.

These are omens of strong ties developing between India and the Soviet Union. While commitments between New Delhi and Moscow do not restrict India from taking initiatives to advance her regional interests, she feels she must continue to rely on Moscow because of the ever-present challenge from China, and because the USSR has now become India's major source for military and economic needs.[14]

The Soviet Union was the only major power that received the news of India's nuclear explosion with approval, even if it was mild. For several years Moscow had made efforts to have New Delhi sign the nuclear nonproliferation treaty. Having failed in this attempt, the Soviet leadership proceeded to assure Mrs. Gandhi that with India's successful test the two nations could carry out joint experiments in further development of nuclear energy for peaceful uses.

India's leadership will never tolerate the status of a Soviet satellite. But superpower rivalry in the Indian Ocean, and the announcement in February, 1975, that the United States has lifted the arms embargo against Pakistan, narrows the options for security-conscious India. If the United States must build Pakistan militarily again because of U.S. concerns in the Middle East, then India will remain alienated. Since the U.S. will not contemplate any action in defense of the subcontinent that could be interpreted by China as directed against her, India cannot be expected to loosen her ties with the Soviet Union, which has become the anchor of her defense against a superior military power.

India and the United States

At the time of Indian independence, there prevailed a belief that the common cultural values and political ideals of India and America provided a natural background for lasting friendship. But this proved to be more a romantic notion than a real one. Conflict of interest between the two surfaced as early as 1948.

From 1949 onward India used the United Nations as a forum to attack Western colonialism and press for an end to all colonial rule in Asia and Africa. Despite her dislike for colonialism as such, the U.S. defended France, Portugal, the Netherlands, and the Union of South Africa in the interest of building a united Western front against the rising danger of Communist expansion in the post-World War II period. In the 1950s the United States moved swiftly to establish military alliances with the aim of containing Communism within "prescribed" boundaries. India condemned these alliances as a threat to world peace and issued a call to the newly born Asian and African states to shun all military blocs. Moreover, India felt that the United States had struck a direct blow at her when the U.S. and Pakistan signed a bilateral military treaty in 1954.

This treaty enabled the U.S. to have access to strategic bases in northwest Pakistan wherefrom American U2 spy missions could be flown over the Soviet Union. But India saw the U.S.-Pakistan alliance as a failure on the part of U.S. to give credit to India's moral leadership and her peace efforts. India also felt that the U.S.-Pak military treaty reduced India's influence on the subcontinent by strengthening her only rival in the region. In addition, India was convinced that Pakistan would use her new military capability to settle the Kashmir issue which had remained since partition a constant source of hostility between the two countries. From the Indian point of view, then, in executing the military treaty the United States had openly declared that her interests coincided with those of Pakistan.

Nineteen sixty-two offered an opportunity for a redefinition of Indo-American relations. The clash with China over India's northern border resulted in a humiliating defeat for India. Nehru turned toward the U.S.A., Britain and the USSR for military assistance to bolster India's defenses. Because of the U.S. anti-Chinese posture at the time, Washington readily obliged, even over strong protests from Pakistan. But before India could become militarily tied to the U.S., America refused to give India supersonic aircraft, air-to-air missiles, and heavy tanks. India realized that she could secure only limited assistance from the U.S. In her view this was another signal that the U.S. continued to give preference and priority to Pakistan.

The 1965 Indo-Pak war brought an end to military and economic aid to India. Greater U.S. involvement in Viet Nam and India's unrestrained criticism of it only widened the breach. The Indo-Pak war of 1971 and President Nixon's strong support of General Yahya Khan's regime in the revolt in East Pakistan dealt the final blow to any chance of improvement in Indo-U.S. relations.

Secretary of State Henry Kissinger made it known to the policy planning staff that President Nixon wanted to "tilt in favor of Pakistan" even as publicly the U.S. attempted to display a posture of impartiality. It was conveyed to India that the U.S.A. would not wage policies which would lead to the overthrow of President Yahya Khan. But after December 3, when the war began, the U.S. government cast off all pretenses and came out openly against India. The American Ambassador to the U.N., George Bush, accused India of committing aggression. American arms were dispatched to Pakistan directly from the U.S.A., as well as through third countries such as Iran, Jordan, and Saudi Arabia. Kissinger has been quoted as saying: "The President does not want to be even-handed. The President believes that India is the attacker." At one point it appeared that the United States was preparing for direct involvement. On December 15, 1971, Indian newspapers revealed that President Nixon had ordered the nuclear armed aircraft carrier Enterprise to sail from Viet Nam into the Bay of Bengal. Jack Anderson, Washington columnist, says that this provocative naval deployment was intended (a) to compel India to divert both ships and planes to shadow the task force; (b) to weaken India's blockade against East Pakistan; (c) possibly to divert the Indian aircraft carrier Vikrant from its military mission, and (d) to force India to keep planes on defense alert, thus reducing their operations against Pakistani ground troops.[15] But this intended show of force proved meaningless. Pakistani forces had surrendered before the American Navy reached its target, and so it changed course. Nonetheless, President Nixon's actions exacerbated the already strained relations between India and the U.S.

John Connally, President Nixon's special emissary, visited New Delhi in July, 1972, to discuss Indo-U.S. relations. In replying to certain questions from the press he said: "The United States has no desire to inject herself into the affairs of the subcontinent." Commenting in specific on Indo-U.S. relations, he observed that American criticism of Indian actions in Bangladesh was far less strident than the Indian criticism of U.S. actions in Vietnam. "We condemned India far less than India has been condemning us." To the question regarding the prospects of U.S. aid to India, his answer was short. "My mission here is not to discuss aid."[16]

On her part Prime Minister Gandhi demonstrated India's independence, and the everpresent feeling that the U.S. has never treated the nations of Asia on an equal footing, when addressing a session of the One-Asia Assembly in New Delhi on February 6, 1973. She said:

> Indian tradition has always spoken of one world—I have grown up in this belief and I abhor chauvinistic nationalism or racialism of any color and type but I would like to ask a question. Would this sort of war or the

savage bombing which has taken place in Viet Nam have been tolerated for so long had the people been European?[17]

When India exploded a nuclear device in 1974, the United States was especially critical of the Indian action. The U.S. response can be primarily attributed to their long-held belief that the biggest gap in the chain reaction of proliferation was from the fifth to the sixth nuclear power. "From sixth to the sixteenth the progression might be rapid," was the general belief of the American scholars.

No amount of reassurance from New Delhi that the test was conducted to explore the use of nuclear energy for peaceful purposes seemed sufficent to calm the voices that expressed dismay, disappointment and anger.

Nonetheless, when it was announced that Kissinger would visit India in October, 1974, spokesmen of goodwill on both sides expressed satisfaction that after a long cold spell a positive step was finally being taken to repair relations between the two largest democracies of the world.

During his three-day visit Kissinger held extensive talks with Prime Minister Gandhi and External Affairs Minister Chavan. At the end of his stay all seemed ready to admit that Kissinger had opened a new chapter in Indo-U.S. relations. A careful scrutiny of the statements made by the secretary on key issues, however, reveals that on some vital matters the two nations are still far apart.

Kissinger publicly went out of his way to assure India's leadership that Washington did not oppose or resent New Delhi's close ties with Moscow. He also pleased the public and the policymakers by stating that the United States recognized India's major role in the affairs of the subcontinent. He added that there was no attempt on the part of the U.S. to equate Pakistan with India. On the second day of his stay Kissinger and Chavan signed an agreement establishing a joint Indo-U.S. Commission which would probe the possibilities of increasing future trade and economic cooperation between the two states.[18]

Kissinger's comments pertaining to India's nuclear explosion were discreet. In a speech before the Indian Council of World Affairs, he let it be known that Washington accepted India's assurances that she had no intention of developing nuclear weapons. But he did suggest that India must observe restraint and caution in its policy of exporting nuclear technology. He said:

> The United States is of the view that countries capable of exporting nuclear technology should agree to common restraints on a multilateral basis which would further the peaceful, but inhibit the military uses of nuclear power. We take seriously India's affirmation that it has no intention to develop nuclear weapons. But India of course has the

capability to export nuclear technology; it therefore has an important role in this multilateral endeavor.[19]

But when it came to two issues critical to India, Kissinger was cautious and noncommittal in his response. In reply to the question of whether the U.S. would resume sending military supplies to Pakistan, the secretary of state responded that there was no intention of encouraging an arms race in the region. However, he refused to give any assurance that the arms embargo against Pakistan would not be lifted.

Kissinger made no remarks about the naval base the U.S. is building in the Indian Ocean. In conversations between the secretary and the Indian officials, both sides were reported to have avoided bringing up the touchy subject for discussion.

On February 24, 1975, to India's shock and dismay, the United States lifted the arms embargo against Pakistan. This led India to conclude that even if the Kissinger visit did open up a dialogue between New Delhi and Washington, the strategic concerns of the two are still at variance, and the two nations will remain divided for some time to come.

It is of crucial importance to India that Pakistan's military strength not rise above a certain level. In addition to the unresolved Kashmir issue, Pakistan now holds another grudge against India. For Pakistan, New Delhi bears the sole responsibility for the severence of East Pakistan. This makes India edgy, and certain that any boost in Pakistan's military capability would tempt her to engage India in another military confrontation.

Arms for Pakistan is a highly sensitive issue for India. New Delhi has repeatedly approached Washington on this matter. Uncertainty surrounded the U.S. attitude until the announcement in February. Just before leaving his post in December, 1974, the then U.S. Ambassador to India Daniel Moynihan was pressed for a statement on the issue by the reporters. His response was sharp:

> I am enough of a professor of government to know that some things sink in pretty slow, but what in the hell do we have to do?
>
> We are the only country in the world which does not sell arms to South Asia that has any arms to sell. . . .
>
> We are the only one. And we've had the policy in effect since 1965 . . . and yet continually we are asked whether we are going to stop arms to South Asia.
>
> We adopted this policy with the expectation that it would be met with approval in the region to which it has applied, and approval at least involves some measure of acknowledgment. If there are those who like the policy and who approve it and want it to persist, thoughtful persons might make some effort to acknowledge that it exists.

> If a policy designed to win a measure of approval wins none, then it clearly is a failed policy. I don't think this is a failed policy, but I hope it does not become one.[20]

Ambassador Moynihan's observations have lost meaning. India's fears have been renewed. Pakistan's Premier Bhutto's visit to Washington in February, 1975, was far more successful in this regard than all the presentations made before the U.S. government by leaders of India.

It is clear that the U.S. security interests continue to warrant military support of Pakistan. India's leadership perceives this as a constant irritant to stability on the subcontinent, and a factor in Pakistan's past noncompromise in normalization of relations.

As mentioned earlier, New Delhi and Washington are also at loggerheads over counterinterests in the Indian Ocean. The U.S. Congress recently appropriated $29 million to build the first permanent U.S. naval base in the Indian Ocean. In a confidential memo to the Congressional leaders, the State Department said:

> In our judgment, an adequate U.S. presence in the Indian Ocean provides a clear signal to the Soviets of our resolve to insure a credible military capability there.... The opening of the Suez Canal will obviously increase the Soviet ability... to show force to influence events where major U.S. interests are at stake.[21]

This has provided the Navy the opportunity to ask for a permanent base in the Indian Ocean, because maintaining ships in this area with logistic support coming from the Subic Bay in the Philippines is considered impractical.

It is expected that Diego Garcia will be turned into a base with a harbor to receive nuclear submarines, and runways to accommodate all types of U.S. planes. It will also have fuel and storage facilities for both ships and planes.

Some congressional representatives are of the opinion that Diego Garcia is bound to become one of the major American naval bases abroad, and the $29 million appropriation is only an initial investment. This is exactly what the littoral states in the area fear. India has been joined in her protest by Malaysia, Indonesia, Australia, New Zealand, and Sri Lanka. It was Sri Lanka's representative who introduced a resolution in the United Nations in 1971 that asked that the Indian Ocean be declared a "Zone of Peace." Both the Soviet Union and the United States have ignored all protests.

It is interesting to note that Ambassador Moynihan said during a press conference in New Delhi on December 13, 1973, that American ships had the right of passage on the high seas and the U.S. would assert that right. He also stated that the "Indian Ocean, ranging from Cape Town to Singapore, was too large an expanse of sea to be ignored."[22]

Apparently the oil crisis has created new American interests in the Middle East and a compelling reason for the United States to stay in the Indian Ocean. India considers the presence of the superpowers a potential threat to the peace of the area. She is also fearful that a possible future conflict between the giant nations will drag in all the littoral states. Already the Soviet Union is pressuring India for a naval base. While India has refused to grant the concession thus far, increased American activity makes it more difficult for India to deny the Soviets this privilege. Resumption of U.S. military aid to Pakistan served as a reminder that the Indo-Soviet security treaty must remain a bulwark of India's defense. Thus India and the U.S. are at odds again. India is fearful that she will be sucked into the Soviet orbit, not by design but more as a consequence of superpower rivalries.

This seems ironic when one considers the fact that until the mid-1960s India ranked first among the developing states receiving economic aid from the United States. Between 1952 and 1965 India received assistance, mostly in the form of loans, of approximately $10 billion. In hopes of creating an atmosphere for improved relations, Ambassador Moynihan worked out an arrangement in June, 1974, whereby Washington agreed to turn over to New Delhi rupees worth $2 billion to be diverted toward several economic development projects in India. The U.S. came to own this amount of Indian currency as a payment for food grains that were shipped to India under Public Law 480 in the 1960s. Also, food credits to India that were terminated by the U.S. in 1971 were restored in December, 1974. As a result India received a loan of nearly $60 million to allow her to purchase 300,000 tons of U.S. wheat, at a time when India was facing severe food shortages. These examples highlight the fact that while economic factors should have pushed India and the United States together, diverse security interests have torn them apart.

There are no signs on the horizon that forecast a radical change in Indo-U.S. relations in the near future. In addition to concerns associated with the Middle East oil problem, détente with the Soviet Union and China appears to be the overwhelming influence on U.S. policy. Inasmuch as India does not figure prominently in this new "balance of power" equation, America's policymakers are not dissatisfied with the situation as it stands. This U.S. posture of semi-indifference works to India's disadvantage especially as far as her economic development is concerned. But the stability on the Indian subcontinent seems to satisfy the interests and desires of the three superpowers at the present time.

Notes

[1] *Indian Parliamentary Debates*, Vol. VI, No. 17, December 6, 1950.
[2] *Lok Sabha Debates*, Vol. 5, No. 70 (May 15, 1954), cols. 7495–96.
[3] *India-China Border Dispute* (March 31, 1959–December 17, 1959), Information Service of India, Embassy of India, Washington, D.C., p. 4.
[4] At a press conference in Mussoorie, India, on June 20, 1959, the Dalai Lama revealed that when he had visited India in 1956 he had given thought to not returning to Tibet as a protest against the oppressive policies pursued by representatives of the Chinese government in Tibet. However, Nehru persuaded him to return, saying that the Chinese had given assurances to Nehru that the situation would be eased if the Dalai Lama returned home.
[5] The border between India and the "Tibetan region of China" is 2,500 miles long. Most of the border is undemarcated and in places it defies demarcation because the mountainous territory is very rugged. India claims that the McMahon Line established the Sino-Indian frontier. The McMahon Line was decided upon by a tripartite agreement between British India, Tibet, and China at the Simla Conference of 1913–14. The People's Republic of China refuses to recognize the McMahon Line, calling it a manifestation of British imperialism. China has pushed forward and occupied territory behind the traditional Sino-Indian frontier, in the northwest as well as in the northeast. In the northwest portion China has built a road linking Sinkiang with Tibet. This road passes through Ladakh, traditionally claimed by India as her territory. It has to be noted that China's representative at the Simla Conference initialed the agreement. But the agreement was never ratified by the Chinese government.
[6] This episode has been dealt with in extensive detail by several authors. But two books with totally opposite viewpoints are worthy of note for their exposure of "inside information" and meticulous coverage of all relevant facts. The two are: Neville Maxwell, *India's China War* (Bombay: Jaico Publishing House, 1970) and B. N. Mullik, *The Chinese Betrayal* (New Delhi: Allied Publisher, 1971).
[7] As quoted by Maxwell in *India's China War*, p. 361.
[8] *The Making of India's Foreign Policy*, p. 248.
[9] *International Affairs*, Vol. 7–12, Published by All Union Society, Moscow, July, 1969, p. 21.
[10] *India News*, October 10, 1969.
[11] Quoted in: S. R. Chowdhury, *The Genesis of Bangladesh*. (New York: Asia Publishing House, 1972), p. 264.
[12] *The Statesman Weekly* (Calcutta), February 17, 1973.
[13] *The Statesman Weekly* (Calcutta), February 24, 1973.
[14] The Soviet Union is now India's second largest trading partner. In the wake of the Indo-Pak war of 1971, the U.S. stopped all nonproject assistance to India. This assistance permitted India to finance the bulk of raw material, fertilizer, newsprint and nonferrous metal imports. India is now expecting to secure these from the USSR and East European countries. India's trade with the Eastern Bloc countries is expected to rise by 30 percent during the coming year. India has already signed agreements with Poland, Czechoslovakia and Rumania to fulfill her needs.
[15] Jack Anderson, *The Anderson Papers* (New York: Random House, 1973), p. 263.
[16] As reported in *London Times*, July 6, 1972.
[17] *India News*, Washington, D.C., February 16, 1973.

[18] *The Statesman Weekly* (Calcutta), November 2, 1974.
[19] "Toward a Global Community: The Common Cause of India and America," Speech by Secretary of State, Bureau of Public Affairs, Dept. of State, Washington, D.C., November 4, 1974, p. 5.
[20] *Los Angeles Times*, December 16, 1974.
[21] As quoted in *The New Republic*, March 9, 1974, p. 7.
[22] *The Statesman Weekly* (Calcutta), December 15, 1973.

Epilogue

India's foreign policy today is guided more by security considerations than by any other set of factors. The experience of four wars has made India highly conscious of her defense. Mrs. Gandhi will never admit nor proclaim that "power lies in the barrel of a gun," but the thrust of her new foreign policy is toward strengthening India's strategic security by means quite different from those employed in the past.

India's new policy approach is emphatically regional in character. She seeks to create a situation wherein no state or combination of states will rise as a counterpower to her in South and Southeast Asia. The task has by no means been accomplished with the splitting of Pakistan and the creation of the new state of Bangladesh, or the incorporation of Sikkim into the Indian Union, or the detonation of a nuclear device. One can say that a change in direction has created a new set of problems for Indian foreign policy. Whether India will succeed in realizing internal stability as well as subcontinental balance in the future will depend upon how Indian leadership meets the challenge ahead.

India's enhanced military capability is proving to be a mixed blessing in view of other parallel developments. If India feels satisfied that the possibility of an attack from Pakistan has been reduced, recent Indian actions vis-à-vis Sikkim have increased the fear on the part of such states as Nepal, Bhutan, and the new state of Bangladesh that internal disruption or assumption of power by a regime considered potentially hostile to Indian interests could lead to direct intervention and even a takeover by India. While the Indian government recognizes that such an adventurous course would spell disaster for the nation, and restraint observed by India in the past clearly indicates no intentions of this sort in the future, the governments of the many neighboring states do not rest easy. Their fears are not allayed by the repeated assurances of the Indian leadership. This opens up the prospect of their courting the Chinese as a counterweight against India, which in turn manifests the perennial dangers of Chinese involvement in South Asia as long as Sino-Indian relations remain unfriendly.

China continues to conduct anti-Indian propaganda among the Third World countries. The intense level of this campaign at times suggests that China still considers India as an irritating element in the Chinese drive for carving a sphere of influence among the underdeveloped societies of Asia and Africa. Chinese and Indian border patrols clashed in the eastern Himalayas as recently as November, 1975. Four Indian soldiers were killed in the clash. India did not react strongly to this incident. It was, however, a reminder for her that China feels free to use force against her at will. It was a signal that, be it to humiliate India subsequent to her nuclear detonation or for any other reason, China would not hesitate to enter the South Asian scene. China resisted the temptation of coming to Pakistan's assistance in 1965 and 1971, primarily due to fear of American and Soviet intervention. But this situation can change with the vagaries of Sino-American and Soviet-American détente, and Sino-Soviet hostility.

It does not come as a total surprise that India's close friendship with the Soviet Union is raising a number of problems with which Indian foreign policymakers must reckon in the future. The Indo-Soviet security treaty was signed under extenuating circumstances. But in subsequent years some key issues have surfaced which will not permit India to rest easy until she can find a way out of her increasing reliance on the Soviet Union for defense and economic development. Peking is convinced that Moscow signed the defense pact with New Delhi in order to encircle China; further, that India has become a party to Soviet designs against China. Therefore, she is not prepared to seek rapprochement with India unless the government in New Delhi either renounces the treaty or takes diplomatic initiatives which would reduce the significance and the impact of the treaty. Given the mistrustful mutual relationship with

China and Pakistan in the recent past, India finds it very difficult to take any action that could prove to be a grave security risk. Even though New Delhi recognizes that settlement of disputes with China and Pakistan is the most significant key to subcontinental stability in the future, the Russian connection is proving to be a barrier in the path of possible Sino-Indian accord.

In addition to boosting the military capability of India, the Indo-Soviet agreement has paved the way for major economic ties between India and Russia. In the short run both sides seemed assured of great mutual benefit. The American tilt in favor of Pakistan in 1971 alienated India's policymakers to the point where they were eager to reduce reliance on American aid to the minimum. Also they saw little hope that Washington would continue its policy of major economic assistance to underdeveloped nations of Asia, since the emphasis appeared to be on disengagement from the area. Therefore, turning toward the Russians for increased economic aid seemed logical. From the Soviet point of view participation in Indian economic development could only lead to increased Soviet influence in India at the grass roots level. This opened up the possibility that the Indian political and cultural patterns could be affected at the very base. Moreover, New Delhi's heightened dependence on Moscow in effect made India a Russian ally in opposing Chinese ideological and political ambitions. Russia was ready to try the experiment. In 1974, however, Soviet economy was itself suffering severe strains. While the oil crisis increased India's difficulties and thus her economic aid demands, the Soviet Union found that India was becoming an increasing economic burden. Moscow could neither supply the amount of aid nor the favorable financial terms sought by India on the basis of their "special relationship." While the Indian government does not say it publicly, it is widely reported that Soviet aid is well below commitment levels. On its part Moscow is not wholly satisfied with the organizational and management ability of the Indians.

Rapid economic development is necessary for internal stability in India. Also her newly found confidence in her military capability rests on it. As long as greater self-sufficiency is not achieved, India will have to turn to outside sources, other than the Soviet Union, for sustained economic growth. The United States and Japan stand out as the nations with the ability to render the kind of help India needs. The pattern of Indo-American relations in the last few years does not suggest any enthusiasm on the part of Washington to reinstitute the economic aid levels to India that existed in the 1950s. To a degree American government is satisfied that this burden has been shifted to Russian shoulders. While the United States has by no means left the Asian scene, her strategy has changed. Having succeeded in exploiting the rift between the two Communist giants, China and Russia, Washington is cultivating friendly relations with China with the objective of building her as an effective counterpower to the Soviet Union in Asia. Support for Pakistan continues to hold great attraction for Washington, partially due to Pakistan's newfound friendship with China. This damages India's chances of receiving massive support from America. Bonds of friendship and cooperation between India and Russia are no help—they simply confirm the belief in Washington that nourishing the Indian cause is an unnecessary luxury.

As the only Asian nation that stands equal in economic achievements with the highly industrialized nations of the West, Japan is at once the envy and the hope of every other non-Communist Asian state. Can India draw upon the industrial resources of Japan to resolve her economic dilemma? While there is no easy answer, clearly India believes that Japan could prove to be the most significant force for future economic help as well as possible security arrangements in South and Southeast Asia. The current leadership in India has made many an overture to draw Japan to the vertex of Asian politics. Japan's response has been cautious; as long as the American-Japanese security treaty remains the sole bulwark of Japan's defense, she cannot be expected to play a prominent or independent role in Asian economic and security matters. Presently Japan finds her relationship with the West best served by pursuing a policy of detachment. The World War II legacy also remains somewhat of a barrier preventing Japan from making bold gestures calculated toward Asian leadership. Nonetheless, considering the options available, strong economic ties with Japan as well as regional security pacts in South and Southeast Asia offer the best hope for India in terms of realizing her objectives of subcontinental stability and security. Apparently this cannot be accomplished without agreement among the superpowers.

Problems of Indian defense do not appear as grave today as they were during the first three decades of Indian independence. But the problems of building a healthy economy and internal cohesion continue to be severe. India's economic viability and internal stability will depend much upon the content of her foreign policy as well as her ability to survive the thrust of superpower rivalries in the years ahead. Prime Minister Nehru struggled hard to escape superpower influence through nonalignment. But Prime Minister Gandhi seems aware that where superpower rivalry is concerned you cannot escape it—you must manipulate it. How well India's leadership does that is the test of future Indian foreign policy.

Appendix

Foreign Policy-Related Statements
from the Election Manifesto of the
Indian National Congress (N, the
Ruling Party), dated 1972.

Our Foreign Policy

Our foreign policy reflects our commitment to democracy, secularism and socialism and follows Jawaharlal Nehru's concept of non-alignment. The basic element of that policy is the maintenance of our own independent judgment in each instance in accordance with the merits of each case and our own national interests. That we have been able to assist in the emergence of a secular, socialist and democratic Bangla Desh is in itself a tribute to the principles to which we have adhered. By continuing to adhere to those principles, we hope to help our region and the world at large in the maintenance of peace and the expansion of areas of international cooperation.

During the period of trial through which we have recently passed, the Soviet Union and other socialist countries as well as some Asian and African, Latin American and European countries, notably U.K. and France, have helped us in different ways. Our relations with the Soviet Union have been further strengthened and consolidated by the Treaty of Peace, Friendship and Cooperation which we signed with them.

As long as effective economic self-reliance is not achieved, it is likely that attempts will be made in the realm of international relations to exploit any weaknesses. In the past, we have been able to resist and frustrate such pressures by summoning every ounce of our will and energy. Self-reliance is the economic counterpart of political independence and its achievement will deter other powers from the temptation of attempting to put pressure on us.

We are determined that India's strength and size shall never become a cause of apprehension to any of our neighbours. We are pledged not to interfere in the internal affairs of our neighbours in any way but to live with all countries in a spirit of co-existence, equality and mutual respect. We reject not only Great Power chauvinism but also the doctrines of spheres of influence and balance of power.

To the new State of Bangla Desh, born out of sacrifice and dedication to freedom, we offer friendship and cooperation. We say to the people of Pakistan that India wishes to live in peace and amity with them. Peace and security can be achieved only through cooperation and not through confrontation. All the nations of our region have one supreme challenge, the eradication of poverty. Let us work together to conquer this common enemy.

Our admiration for the heroic people of North Vietnam in their long struggle has been re-emphasized by our recent decision to establish closer diplomatic ties between our two countries.

During these last months, certain countries have chosen to remain indifferent to the cause of human justice involved in the struggle of the people of Bangla Desh. But it is our earnest hope that these Governments will soon recognise the realities. The people of India greatly appreciate the sympathy and support given by the freedom loving peoples of the world and the international news media.

Conclusion

The struggle of the people of Bangla Desh and the response of the Government and people of India under the leadership of Prime Minister, Smt. Indira Gandhi, the victory of our Armed Forces and our para-military forces and the sacrifices made by them, once again underline the soundness of the principles of democracy, secularism and socialism which have animated the Indian National Congress during the national freedom struggle. Today these principles provide the only basis for consolidating our freedom, our democracy and our economic future.

The Congress is the only Party which can place its programme before the people with a sense of responsibility. It is the only Party which can give a unified lead to the country by establishing strong and effective Governments in the States and at the Centre which are committed to implement this far-reaching socio-economic programme, aimed to restructure our economy on the basis of self-reliance.

The Congress pledges itself anew to these challenging tasks, to a socialist revolution which is peaceful and democratic and embraces all our people and permeates all spheres of national life. The Congress is the only Party which has the capacity to achieve such a social revolution.

The people have the power. In March 1971, they used it to reject the reactionaries and communalists of the right and the extremists, who resort to violence and disorder and try to disrupt the forces of progress in the garb of left slogans. Now the people are called upon once again to choose and again we appeal to the people to give us their mandate.

We reiterate our objective: *Poverty must go. Disparity must diminish. Injustice must end.* These are but essential steps towards our ultimate goal—the goal of an India which is united and strong, an India which, living up to its ancient and enduring ideals, yet is modern in thought and achievement, meeting the future with vision and confidence.

Foreign Policy-Related Statements from the Election Manifesto of the Indian National Congress (O), dated 1971.

The Congress will never tolerate occupation of Indian territories by foreign powers.

The Congress will restore the balance in India's foreign policy and make it once again truly and dynamically non-aligned. While we shall maintain the existing ties of friendship, it will be our special endeavour to revive relations that have been weakened by the present government. India offers friendship to, and seeks cooperation with all countries. The Congress will lay special emphasis on our relations with countries in South-East Asia, West Asia and other regions of strategic and economic importance to India. The Congress will constantly endeavour to foster understanding with

Pakistan whenever and wherever the opportunities arise. We seek partnership in peace and progress with all our neighbours.

Foreign Policy-Related Statements from the Election Manifesto of the Communist Party of India, dated January, 1971

Electoral Aims of Communist Party in the Sphere of Foreign Policy

The strengthening of India's foreign policy of peace and non-alignment based firmly on anti-colonialism and anti-imperialism and on friendship and cooperation with the Soviet Union and other socialist countries.

More effective stand against racialism and break with the British Commonwealth.

Full diplomatic recognition to the Democratic Republic of Vietnam (DRV), German Democratic Republic (GDR), Democratic People's Republic of Korea (DPRK) and upgrading of the Indian missions in these friendly countries to ambassadorial level.

Recognition of the Provisional Revolutionary Government of the Republic of South Vietnam.

Upholding of the Tashkent Declaration and constant effort to normalise Indo-Pak relations in the Tashkent spirit.

All possibilities are to be explored for breaking the present deadlock in India's relations with the People's Republic of China.

Strengthening of India's solidarity with Afro-Asian countries, especially with the UAR and other Arab peoples defending their freedom against Israeli aggressor and US imperialism.

Uninhibited trade with the Democratic Republic of Vietnam (DRV), Cuba and other friendly countries.

Effective measures to defend national interest against neo-colonialist drives and pressures.

Foreign Policy-Related Statements from the Election Manifesto of the Praja Socialist Party, dated January 2, 1971

Foreign and Defence Policy

The PSP believes in a dynamic, independent foreign policy that upholds the peace and freedom of all nations but remains deeply rooted in our national interests. The Party is opposed to all types of military alliances, which invariably lead to entanglements with the politics of Big Powers. While adhering to a policy of genuine non-alignment, the Party will not refuse to judge every international event on its merits. The PSP will always express its solidarity with the struggle of the colonial people who are suffering under imperialist and neo-imperialist regimes.

The PSP wants to strengthen the United Nations as an instrument of collective security. The party favours forging of close links with Asian countries against Chinese expansionism.

The PSP will never allow the Indian Ocean to be exploited by the Big Powers for their domination or political interference.

The PSP feels that friendly relations with the Arab world are compatible with similar relations with Israel. The PSP welcomes the victory of the forces of progress and secularism in the general elections in Pakistan and hopes that it will pave the way for friendly relations between India and Pakistan.

For strengthening the defence of our country in the face of the threat to our freedom from the aggressors, the PSP would strive to be self-sufficient in conventional as well as nuclear weapons—starting with tactical nuclear weapons.

The defence effort will be broad-based by ensuring the widest association of the people with it. The efforts of our Armed Forces to defend our borders will be supplemented by establishing co-operative agricultural communities on our frontiers providing a second line of defence.

Kashmir

The PSP reiterates its earlier stand that after the adoption of the Constitution by the Constituent Assembly of Jammu and Kashmir, the entire State has become an integral part of India and the accession of Kashmir is final and irrevocable. The PSP will prevent the misuse of Article 370 of the Constitution, which is intended to protect the special interests of the people of Jammu and Kashmir.

Foreign Policy-Related Statements from Resolutions adopted by the General Council of the Swatantra Party, dated September 17–18, 1971.

Bangla Desh

The General Council of the Swatantra Party views with grave concern the present position in regard to the refugees from Bangla Desh. The Government keeps reiterating its determination to see that the refugees return to Bangla Desh but has taken no steps yet which could in any sense be considered as designed to achieve their return.

Since the Government itself claims that the Treaty with Soviet Russia was entered into for other and more long term reasons, the present situation cannot but cause deep anxiety to the people of this country.

The Swatantra Party deplores the attitute of all those countries who continue to give help, aid and military hardware to Pakistan and who do not grasp the significance of giving succour to Pakistan and its effects on peace in the sub-continent.

On the other hand, we see that the flow of refugees into India is incessant; and we see on the other, partly because of the burdens imposed by the refugees mainly because of the continued pursuit of unrealistic economic policies, that the country's economy far from growing is threatening to come to a grinding halt.

The General Council of the Swatantra Party, therefore urges the Government to put an end to its policy of drift and set a time limit within which it should call upon all the foreign powers particularly the Soviet Union, who have been counselling restraint, that after the expiry of the time limit if they have not succeeded in creating conditions for the refugees to go back, it will take firm steps on its own, to resolve the problem of refugees.

Indo-Soviet Treaty

The General Council of the Swatantra Party views with concern the conclusion of the Indo-Soviet Treaty. The Council apprehends that the long term effects of the Treaty will be injurious to the free way of life of the Indian people and to our country's international relations and prestige.

The Treaty fetters India's freedom of action and narrows the options open to this country at a time when international relationships are in a state of flux. The Treaty, which threatens to reduce India to a position of a satellite, will needlessly narrow the number of India's friends and tend to isolate it.

The effects of the Treaty on the domestic front will be equally deleterious. It will facilitate further infiltration into the cultural and economic life of our country. It will accelerate the threat to our Constitution and the Fundamental Rights of the citizen already posed by the 24th and 25th Constitutional Amenedment Bills. The fact that the Indian Government which has concluded the Treaty contains several ex-Communists and fellow travellers of international communism gives the Treaty a particularly dangerous character.

Foreign Policy-Related Statements from the Election Manifesto of the Jana Sangh Party, dated January, 1972.

For the first time since independence, elections to a majority of the State Assemblies are going to be held separately from those for the Parliament. For the first time, the electorate has an opportunity of exercising its franchise on the basis, mainly, of State level issues closer to the people. Now, therefore, is the time for people to judge whether the party in power has lived up to its professions or betrayed the trust reposed in it.

The Ruling Congress wants the vote for itself in the name of victory and stability. Fact is that it can claim neither. What we have just won was a glorious national victory made possible by our gallant forces. Indeed, had the Congress (R) heeded Jana Sangh's demand to recognise Bangla Desh in early summer, we could have stopped the genocide and defeated the Pakistani army before it had reinforced itself. Even now, judged by official ambiguity about the liberated territories, recovery of reparations and trial of war-criminals, the fear is that Congress will let down the country after the elections are safely over.

Index

Abdullah, Sheikh, 103
Abu Dhabi, 35
Afghanistan, 13, 102, 120
Africa, 4, 51, 52, 66, 81, 142
Afro-Asian states, 5, 37, 92, 97, 135, 142
Afro-Asian world, 7, 118, 132, 135
Aksai Chin Road, 15
Albania, 137
Algiers Conference of nonaligned nations, 95
Ali, Mohammed, 107
All India Assoc. of Democratic Lawyers, 82
All India Muslim Legislator's Convention, 82
All India Peace Council, 79, 82, 83
All India Progressive Writer's Assoc., 82
All India Radio, 53
All Jammu and Kashmir National Conference, 103
Amin, Idi, 96
Anderson, Jack, 143
Ansari, M.A., 50

Arab states, 104, 118; Arab-Israeli War, 118
Argentina, 27
Aron, Raymond, 12
Asia, 2, 4, 5, 6, 7, 51, 52, 115, 135, 142; collective security, 139; and Europe, 53
Asian Federation, 54
Asian Relations Conference, 54
Asian states, 3, 152
Asian unity, 48
Ashoka, Emperor, 48
Atlantic Charter, 92
Atom bomb, 14, 60
Atomic Energy of Canada Ltd., 25
Australia, 146
Austria, 4
Awami League Party, 111
Ayub Khan, Mohammed, 63, 107, 108
Ayyanger Committee, 16
Azad, Maulana Abul Kalam, 62
Aziz, Tariq, 119

Baghdad Pact, 5, 117
Bajpai, K. S., 123

161

Balance of power, 13
Bandaranaike, Sirimavo, 98, 127, 128
Bandung Conference, 97, 98, 132
Bangladesh, 7, 21, 30, 37, 38, 105, 109, 110, 112, 113, 114, 115, 116, 117, 136, 140, 143, 150, 151
Bay of Bengal, 143
Bhutan, 121, 122, 123, 124, 151
Bhutto, Z. A., 23, 24, 114, 115, 117, 136, 146
Birendra, Maharaja, 125, 126
Brazil, 27, 28, 35
Brezhnev, Leonid, 41, 139, 141
Britain, 6, 7, 19, 22, 26, 29, 34, 36, 100, 101, 108, 136, 140, 142
British 3, 14; India, 81; Nepali treaty, 124
Buddha, 47
Buddhism, 7, 47, 130
Buddhists, 103; shrines, 99
Bulganin, Nikolai, 5, 139
Burma, 80, 81, 98, 135, 139
Burns, Gen. E. L. M., 26
Bush, George, 143

Cairo Conference of nonaligned nations, 60
Cambodia, 135
Canada, 23, 24, 26, 29
Cape Town, 147
Castro, Fidel, 96
Central Treaty Organization (CENTO), 5
Ceylon, see also Sri Lanka, 81, 98, 127, 135, 138
Chagla, M. C., 66
Chavan, Y. B., 35, 115, 144
Chiang Kai-shek, 93, 131
China, People's Republic of, 1, 5, 6, 7, 8, 13, 15, 16, 22, 26, 27, 31, 36, 38, 43, 55, 94, 102, 108, 113, 116, 121, 124, 125, 126, 130–137, 139, 140, 141, 142, 147, 151, 152, 153
Chinese Communists, 17
Chogyal, 122
Chou En-lai, 97, 125, 132, 134
Chul-ka Sum, 81
Colombo Conference, 127
Colombo Plan, 24, 25, 122
Colombo Powers, 97
Colombo Proposals, 135
Colonialism, 48, 50, 51, 52, 126
Commonwealth, 19, 126
Communism, 4, 138, 142
Communist Party of India (CPI), 65, 79, 83, 131
Congress Party, see Indian National Congress

Connally, John, 143
Cook, Hope, 123
Cunha, Paulo, 101
Czechoslovakia, 63, 104

Dalai Lama, 6, 82, 99, 133
Détente, 9, 96, 139, 147, 151
Dhar, D. P., 69, 70, 110, 141, 151
Diego Garcia, 42, 146
Disarmament, 14
Dulles, John Foster, 59, 91, 101
Dutch-Indonesian conflict, 138

East Asian peoples, 7
East Pakistan, see also Bangladesh, 8, 21, 30, 38, 140, 142
Eastern bloc, 3
Eastern Europe, 35
Egypt, 6, 26, 29, 118, 135
Emergency, state of, 10
Enterprise, U.S. aircraft carrier, 143
Europe, 1, 93; in Asia, 54
European, 4; Europeans, 51; colonies in Asia, 53

Faisal, of Saudi Arabia, 96
Far East, 101
Federation of Indian Chambers of Commerce and Industry (FICCI), 80
Five Year Defense Plan, 19
Ford Foundation, 35
Formosa, 131
France, 6, 19, 22, 26, 27, 101, 140, 142
French enclaves, 76, 100

Gandhi, Mahatma, 2, 13, 47, 54, 92, 96; on nonviolence, 48, 49
Gandhi, Prime Minister Indira, 8, 9, 13, 22, 60, 63, 69, 70, 109, 110, 114, 116, 118, 127, 136, 144; on India's nuclear test, 24, 25, 26, 29, 40; on nonalignment, 96; on nuclear weapons and NPT, 27, 28, 30; on Vietnam, 143; and Congress Party, 77–78; and Indian foreign policy, 150–153
Geneva Conference, 95, 96, 132; Geneva Agreement, 92
German Democratic Republic, 83
Ghana, 135
Goa, 2, 4, 5, 6, 19, 36, 93, 139; Goan crisis, 100–102
Gromyko, Andre, 110

Hangen, Welles, 19
Himalayas, 131
Himalayan border, 4, 18
Hinduism, 7, 47

Hindu Mahasabha, 65
Hiroshima, 29, 31
Hossain, Saddam, 119
Hungarian crisis, 6
Hungary, 104
Hyderabad, 17, 102

Imperialism, 50
India: agriculture, 32; armed forces, 17–21; cabinet and foreign policy 61–63; constituent assembly, 13; constitution, 61, 63, 86; Constitution Amendment Bill, 123; economic capability, 31–36; foreign policy, 1–10, 150–153; GNP, 34; industry, 33; nuclear capability, 22–31; parliament and foreign policy, 63–67; political parties, 73; press, 85–87; public opinion, 83–85; space research program, 39; steel production, 34; and Afghanistan, 120; and Asia, 96–99; and Asianism, 52–55; and Bangladesh, 116–117; and Bhutan, 121–122; and China, 130–137; and Goa, 100–102; and Iran, 119; and Iraq, 119; and Kashmir, 102–105; and Libya, 120; and Middle East, 117–119; and Nepal, 124–126; and Pakistan, 106–116; and Saudi Arabia, 120; and Sikkim, 122–124; and Soviet Union, 137–141; and Sri Lanka, 126–128; and Sudan, 120; and United States, 141–147
Indian communists, 131
Indian Council of World Affairs, 144
Indian minorities, 81, 98
Indian Muslims, 82
Indian National Congress Party, 2, 3, 49, 58, 64, 126, 130, 131; and foreign policy, 74–78
Indian Ocean, 22, 42, 43, 99, 145, 146, 147
Indian Socialist Party, 82
Indians overseas, 127
India-China border clash, 151
India-China border dispute, 15, 133, 134, 135
India-China war, 18, 19, 122, 127, 134, 139
Indo-Burma Immigration Agreement, 80
Indo-Canadian Agreement on nuclear exchange, 25, 26
Indo-Pak war–1947, 15
Indo-Pak war–1965, 16, 20, 136, 142
Indo-Pak war–1971, 16, 21, 30, 85, 139, 142

Indo-Portuguese Treaty, 102
Indo-Soviet Commission on Economic, Scientific and Technical Cooperation, 140
Indo-Soviet Cultural Society, 79, 83
Indo-Soviet Economic Agreement, 42, 140, 141
Indo-Soviet Treaty of Friendship and Cooperation, 8, 9, 37, 96, 109, 110, 136, 137, 139, 147, 151
Indonesia, 35, 52, 54, 95, 97, 135, 139, 146; and Netherlands, 54–55
Indus Waters Treaty, 107
International Bank for Reconstruction and Development, 35, 107
International Conference for World Peace, 53
International Congress against Imperialism, Brussels Conference, 58
International Press Institute, 85
Iran, 29, 33, 35, 118, 143; Shah of, 119
Iraq, 33, 35, 118
Israel, 27, 29, 104

Jan Sangh, 65, 79
Japan, 23, 26, 34, 49, 98, 130, 153
Jha, L. K., 69, 110
Jordan, 118, 143
Junagarh, 17, 102

Kachchative island, 128
Kalimpong, 81, 82
Karen rebels, 98
Kashmir, 2, 3, 4, 5, 7, 15, 17, 20, 36, 63, 93, 114, 116, 139, 142, 145
Katzir, Ephraim, 29
Kaul, Lt. Gen. B. M., 14, 59
Khadafi, Col., 96
Khan, Gen. Yahya, 26, 110, 111, 112, 114, 136, 140, 142, 143
Khan, Liaquat Ali, 103
Khrushchev, Nikita, 5, 101, 138, 139
Kidwai, Rafi Ahmed, 62
King Mahendra, 125
King Tribhuvan, 125
Kissinger, Henry, 9, 22, 110, 115, 143, 144, 145
Koirala, B. P., 125
Korea, 5, 96, 131, 138; Korean war, 4, 59, 92; Korean truce, 131
Kosygin, Aleksei, 108, 139
Krishnamachari, T. T., 62, 63
Kuwait, 35

Ladakh, 15
League of Nations, 12, 53
Libya, 138

Madam Chiang Kai-shek, 131
Malagasy Republic, 35
Malaysia, 99, 146
Mao Tse-tung, 93, 97, 110, 131
Marshal Chen-yi, 134
Mehta, Ashok, 63
Menon, K. P. S., 16, 59
Menon, Mrs. Lakshmani, 67
Menon, V. K. Krishna, 5, 13, 61, 62, 65, 67, 78, 83, 94, 95, 134, 135
Mexico, 35
Middle East, 5, 29, 42, 104, 118, 141, 147
Mookerjee, S. P., 63
Morocco, 52
Moscow Summit, 27
Mountbatten, Lord Louis, 103
Moynihan, Daniel P., 145, 146, 147
Mukti Bahini, 109, 112, 113
Muscat, 35
Muslim nations, 117, 118; Conference at Rabat, 118
Muslims in South Asia, 116

Naga rebels, 98
Nagasaki, 29, 31
Namgyal, King Palden Thondup, 123
Narain, Jaya Prakash, 82
Nassar, Abdel Gamal, 92, 118
Nasseri, Dr. F., 119
Ne Win, 98, 99
Nehru, Jawaharlal, 1, 2, 4, 5, 6, 7, 13, 15, 25, 37, 66, 67, 107, 130, 131, 153; philosophical orientation, 47–55; and Congress Party, 75; as prime minister and foreign minister, 56–60; on Asia, 55; on colonialism, imperialism and racialism, 50–51; on nonalignment, 92–93; on Goa, 100; on Himalayan border states, 121
Neogy, K. C., 63
Nepal, 122, 123, 124, 137, 151; Nepali Congress, 125, 126
Netherlands, 142
Neutral Nations Repatration Commission (NNRC), 5, 59
New Zealand, 146
Nixon, Richard, 29, 42, 110, 142, 143
Nkrumah, Kwame, 92
Nonalignment, 4, 5, 6, 7, 37, 66, 109, 139; in Indian foreign policy, 91–96
Nonviolence, 48, 49
North Vietnam, 83, 99
Northwest frontier, 13
Nuclear device, 9, 16, 137
Nuclear disarmament, 27

Nuclear Nonproliferation Treaty (NPT), 22, 26, 27–28
Nuclear-weapon states, 27, 28

Pakistan, 3, 5, 7, 8, 9, 13, 14, 16, 17, 18, 20, 23, 26, 27, 31, 35, 36, 38, 43, 55, 82, 102, 112, 113, 115, 116, 124, 137, 140, 141, 142, 143, 150, 151, 152, 153; armed forces, 21
Palestine Liberation Organization (PLO), 121
Palestine refugees, 118
Palk Straits, 128
Pan-Arab movement 118
Pan-Islamic movement, 118
Panchsheel, 5, 132
Pandit, Mrs. Vijay Laxami, 94, 138
Pant, Govind Vallabh, 62
Patel, H. M., 14
Patel, Vallabhbhai, 2, 53
Peace Indigo, 38
Philippines, 97, 146
Poland, 138
Portugal, 6, 36, 142; enclaves of, 76, 100
Praja Socialists, 65; Party, 79, 82
Press Trust of India, 87
Princely states of India, 102
Public Law 480, 147
Pushtu speaking people, 120

Quester, George, 30
Quit India Resolution, 131

Racialism 50, 51
Rahman, Sheikh Mujiber, 111, 112, 117
Ram, Jagjivan, 21, 22
Ranadive, 131
Ranas, 124, 125
Rann of Kutch, 107
Reid, Escott, 25
Reuters, 87
Rogers, William, 110
Rumania, 35

Sadaat, Anwar, 96
Salt Talks I, 27
Samyukta Socialist Party, 79
Saudi Arabia, 118, 143
San Francisco Conference on Japanese Peace Treaty, 59
Sastroamidjojo, Ali, 97
Satyagrah, 49
Selassie, Emperor Haile, 96
Sethna, H. N., 40
Sharp, Mitchell, 24
Shastri, Lal Bahadur, 8, 13, 60, 63, 68,

69, 70, 107, 108, 109, 127, 135; on
  NPT, 60; on nonalignment, 107
Sikkim, 123, 137, 150, 151; National
  Assembly of, 123
Simla Agreement, 24, 114
Singapore, 99, 147
Singh, Baldev, 17
Singh, Dinesh, 78
Singh, Kewal, 123
Singh, Swaran, 30, 99
Sinha, Satya Narain, 67
Sinhalese, 126
Sino-Soviet rivalry, 99, 109; border
  clash, 139
Skachkov, 140
Socialist Party, 65
South Africa, 27, 52, 138, 142
South Asia, 5, 8, 21, 23, 31, 43, 105,
  109, 112, 115, 126, 145, 150, 151,
  153
South-West Africa, 138
Southeast Asia, 5, 43, 66, 99, 150, 153;
  Treaty (SEATO), 5, 29, 37, 97, 99
Soviet Academy of Sciences, 39
Soviet Union (USSR), 2, 3, 4, 5, 6, 7, 8,
  9, 15, 19, 20, 22, 26, 30, 34, 36, 37,
  38, 42, 43, 91, 93, 94, 102, 104, 108,
  109, 113, 125, 136, 137, 142, 146,
  147, 151, 152, 153
Sri Lanka, 97, 126, 127, 146
Stalin, Josef, 138
Standstill Agreement, 103
Stevenson III, Adlai E., 29
Subic Bay, 146
Suez crisis, 6, 92, 95, 118
Sukarno, 92
Superpowers, 1, 153
Swatantra Party, 65, 79
Swiss Embassy, 24
Switzerland, 4

Tagore, Rabindranath, 53, 96
Taiwan, 28
Tashkent, 8, 109; Agreement, 104, 108
Tass, 87, 140
Tata Steel Works, 34
Test Ban Treaty, 22
Thailand, 97, 99
Thimayya, Lt. Gen. K. S., 59
Third World, 7, 9, 23, 41, 97, 151
Tibet, 6, 15, 121, 131, 132; refugees,
  81; revolt, 6, 133; Sino-Indian
  agreement on, 132
Tito, Josip B., 92
Treaty of Punakha, 121
Trudeau, Pierre, 26
Tunisia, 52

Turkey, 101
Tyagi, Mahavir, 63

U2 Spy Mission, 142
UAR, see Egypt
U Nu, 92, 98, 99
U Thant, 113
Ukraine, 138
UNESCO, 86
United Nations, 4, 5, 12, 15, 17, 20, 52,
  54, 55, 59, 93, 104, 110, 115, 124,
  126, 132, 136, 138, 142; General
  Assembly, 26, 30, 52, 94, 112, 122;
  Security Council, 15, 23, 28, 54, 95,
  102, 103, 104, 108, 113, 138, 140;
  Trusteeship Council, 52, 138;
  resolution on Indian Ocean, 146
United Press of America, 87
United States, 2, 3, 4, 5, 6, 7, 8, 9, 19,
  20, 22, 26, 28, 29, 30, 36, 37, 42, 43,
  55, 91, 94, 101, 104, 108, 113, 125,
  136, 139, 141, 152, 153; Japan
  Security Treaty, 153; navy, 42, 143;
  Pak Security Treaty, 15, 24, 104,
  107, 139, 142; arms aid to Pakistan,
  115, 145, 147; Atomic Energy
  Commission, 25; military and
  economic aid to India, 142, 143,
  147; Seventh Fleet, 22; and
  colonialism, containment of
  communism and military alliances,
  142; and the Indian Ocean, 146; on
  Indian nuclear test, 144
Universal Postal Union, 122

West Bengal, 8, 110
West Germany, 28, 29, 34
West Pakistan, 8, 30, 36
Western bloc, 3
Western colonialism, 142
Western Europe, 35, 36; tradition of,
  47
Western powers, 101, 102, 104, 113,
  116, 118, 136, 139
Whitehall, 81
World Bank, 35
World Communist Party Conference,
  139
World Powers, 14
World War I, 53
World War II, 4, 13, 16, 33, 49, 52, 53,
  54, 102, 138, 153

Yugoslavia, 28

B&T 840